TIMESAVER FOR EXA

IELTS Reading
(4.0–5.5)

By Julie Moore and Norman Whitby

SCHOLASTIC

Contents

Introduction

Who is this book for?

This book is for teachers of students preparing for the Academic version of the IELTS test who are aiming for a score of 4.0–5.5. It is an ideal supplement to any IELTS preparation coursebook, especially for those new to the exam. The topics and activities reflect those typical of the IELTS Academic test and are designed especially to appeal to young adults. This resource is also suitable for use with students in intermediate classes who wish to begin to develop their academic reading, especially with a view to academic study.

The IELTS test: an overview

The International English Language Testing System (IELTS) is a test that measures the language proficiency of people who want to study or work in environments where English is used as a language of communication. An easy-to-use nine-band scale clearly identifies proficiency level, from non-user (band score 1) through to expert (band score 9).

IELTS is available in two test formats – Academic or General Training – and provides a valid and accurate assessment of the four language skills: listening, reading, writing and speaking. This Timesaver title focuses on the Academic version of the test.

There are four components to the test.

Reading 60 minutes. There are three texts with 40 questions.

Writing 60 minutes. There are two writing Tasks. Task 1 has a minimum of 150 words. Task 2 has a minimum of 250 words.

Listening approximately 30 minutes (plus 10 minutes for transferring answers). There are four sections with 40 questions.

Speaking 11–14 minutes. There are three parts.

Scoring

Each component of the test is given a band score. The average of the four scores produces the overall band score. You do not pass or fail IELTS; you receive a score.

The IELTS scale

Band score	Skill level	Description
9	Expert user	The test taker has fully operational command of the language. Their use of English is appropriate, accurate and fluent, and shows complete understanding.
8	Very good user	The test taker has fully operational command of the language with only occasional unsystematic inaccuracies and inappropriate usage. They may misunderstand some things in unfamiliar situations. They handle complex and detailed argumentation well.
7	Good user	The test taker has operational command of the language, though with occasional inaccuracies, inappropriate usage and misunderstandings in some situations. They generally handle complex language well and understand detailed reasoning.
6	Competent user	The test taker has an effective command of the language despite some inaccuracies, inappropriate usage and misunderstandings. They can use and understand fairly complex language, particularly in familiar situations.
5	Modest user	The test taker has a partial command of the language and copes with overall meaning in most situations, although they are likely to make many mistakes. They should be able to handle basic communication in their own field.
4	Limited user	The test taker's basic competence is limited to familiar situations. They frequently show problems in understanding and expression. They are not able to use complex language.
3	Extremely limited user	The test taker conveys and understands only general meaning in very familiar situations. There are frequent breakdowns in communication.
2	Intermittent user	The test taker has great difficulty understanding spoken and written English.
1	Non-user	The test taker has no ability to use the language except a few isolated words.

For full details on the IELTS test, go to: www.ielts.org

How do I use this book?

The book is divided into 25 lessons. The lessons cover all of the IELTS reading exam skills and are grouped by skill for ease of navigation. Use the lessons to supplement your coursebook by providing extra practice of particular parts of the test or topic areas. The activities also provide thorough practice of exam skills.

- The activities are designed to be teacher-led but are used without separate teacher's notes. Clear instructions are on the pages, which are all photocopiable.

- The reading question type is at the top of every lesson page and in the Exam Focus column on the Contents page, where details of the Exam Skill developed in every lesson can also be found.

- The lessons have been designed to cover approximately one hour of class time, depending on class size and language level.

- The comprehensive answer key at the back of the book provides an explanation of the answers.

- There are reading tips in each lesson to raise students' awareness of the most important strategies for academic reading.

- Some activities ask students to work in pairs or groups to encourage them to engage with the topic of that particular lesson. These can be adapted depending on context and class size.

- There is an **EXAM TASK** in every lesson, which requires students to read a complete IELTS passage and answer a set of questions using the skills they have developed during the lesson. These tasks can be set as timed reading practice in class under exam conditions.

How important are academic reading skills for exam success?

The IELTS test requires candidates to be able to use a wide range of reading skills, including: finding a specific piece of information within a long text; understanding accompanying visuals; understanding how ideas in the text are linked and developed within and between paragraphs; and identifying the writer's overall purpose. This is reflected in the range of questions, which include: short answer questions; identifying information (as in true / false / not given); diagram label completion; matching headings to paragraphs; and multiple choice questions. The activities in this book provide practice of the different question types that students will meet in the exam and aim to develop the different reading skills which they require.

In the IELTS test, candidates are faced with a relatively long text and questions which they must answer within a limited time. It is important for them to realise that they do not need to understand all the words in the text and may not have to read all of it in detail. Their purpose in reading is to extract the information in order to answer the questions. The activities in this book introduce students to this idea by providing analysis and practice of the question types first, so that students are clear about their purpose in reading and can develop the confidence to deal with the text in the way which best matches that purpose.

At least one of the texts in the IELTS exam contains detailed logical argument, and certain question types (e.g. true / false / not given, matching headings and multiple choice) also require students to recognise logical relationships between ideas, such as cause and effect. The activities in this book provide practice in identifying these relationships, as they are expressed both in the questions and the wording in the text.

Another key to obtaining the correct answer in many question types (e.g. short answer questions, gapfill sentences, gapfill summaries) is precision. Where relevant, the activities in this book train students to identify exactly what kind of word or information they need to search for in the text. It introduces techniques which enable them to identify the correct answers by using both grammatical information and meaning and, just as importantly, to discount information in the text which does not match what they are looking for.

Although it is not necessary to understand all the words in a reading text, vocabulary does play a key role in this section of the test. Thus, the lessons include regular tips and activities to develop strategies for working out the meaning of unfamiliar vocabulary, such as by recognising synonyms or understanding affixes. There is also work on understanding frequently used academic vocabulary, such as words and phrases used to describe cause and effect relationships, which is often key to answering questions on a text.

Timesaver series

The Timesaver series provides hundreds of ready-made lessons for all language levels and age groups, covering skills work, language practice and cross-curricular and cross-cultural material. See the full range of print and digital resources at: **www.scholastic.co.uk/elt**

Lighting the Olympic flame

Short answer questions

1 Work in pairs. Make a list of all the international sports competitions that you know. Which ones have you seen live or on TV? Which do you find most exciting?

2 Read the question beginnings (a–h) and match them with TWO possible answers from the box. Which question beginning can have two different meanings?

a) What shape … *circular, square*

b) In which city …

c) In which year …

d) How long …

e) What sort of person …

f) Which metal …

g) What criticism …

h) What was the main purpose of …

Muhammad Ali, 1996 Olympic Games

Beijing   Berlin   circular   dangerous   doctor   educational   four years   gold   iron   1982
poet   1780   square   too expensive   tourist attraction   20 metres

3a Look at the questions and underline the key words or phrases.

1 In which city was the Olympic Flame introduced in modern times?

2 In which year did the torch relay first take place?

3b Compare your answers in pairs. Do the words you chose have opposites? What are they?

4a Scan sections A and B only of the passage and underline the dates and city names.

4b Answer questions 1 and 2 in exercise 3a. Use the information that you underlined in exercise 4a.

4c Read the questions (3–10). Think about the types of answers you need to look for (a time, a date, a number, etc.). Then underline ONE key word that can change the meaning of questions 5 and 6.

3 What source of heat was used to first light the torch in 1936?

4 How was the flame carried to the host city in 1952?

5 How long did the first worldwide torch relay take?

6 When was Olympic cauldron first lit by a woman?

7 What kind of person lit the Olympic cauldron in 1994?

8 How many nations competed in the Olympics in 2012?

9 What criticism was made of the Olympic torch in 2006?

10 What fuel was used for the torch in 1956?

✏ **EXAM TASK: Reading (short answer questions)**

5 Read the complete passage and answer questions 3–10 in exercise 4c. Choose no more than TWO words and/or a number from the passage for each answer.

Exam tip

In the IELTS exam, the answers to a set of short answer questions will appear in the passage in the same order as the questions.

The Olympic torch relay

A The Olympic Flame has long been a feature of the Olympic Games. When the Ancient Greeks held the Games, fires were lit in Athens to mark the start of the competitions and they were kept alight for as long as the Games continued. This tradition was revived for the first time in the 20th century in Amsterdam, during the 1928 Olympics. It has formed part of the ceremony for every Olympic Games held since then.

B Whereas the Olympic Flame is a very old tradition, the idea of holding a torch relay is relatively modern. In this process, a torch is carried around Greece by a number of different runners and then to the city where the Games will be held. It is then used to light the flame there. The first relay was carried out for the Summer Olympics in Berlin in 1936. The flame was lit in Greece by directing sunlight onto the torch with the help of a mirror and then transported over 3,100 kilometres to Berlin.

C Usually the torch is carried on foot, but over the years various methods have been used to move it. The 1952 Games in Helsinki was the first occasion when the flame was taken to its final destination by plane. Then, in 2004, the first global torch relay took place. The torch was lit in Greece on 25 March, and on 4 June started its route across 34 cities on four continents (Australia, Asia, America and Europe). In total, the relay lasted 78 days, covering more than 78,000 kilometres.

D At the end of the relay, the flame is transferred from the torch to a cauldron* at the stadium where the Games are to be held. The person who does this is usually a sports celebrity. The first well-known athlete to light the cauldron was the Finnish runner Paavo Nurmi, in 1952. Other famous people have included the boxing champion Muhammad Ali (1996). Enriqeta Basilio, the

Mexican athletics champion, was the first female carrier to transfer the flame in Mexico City in 1968. In 1994 the Olympic flame was brought into the stadium by a ski jumper who gave it to the Crown Prince of Norway. In the 2012 Olympics in London, the organisers decided that the cauldron should be the centre of attention, rather than the torch. It was made of 204 pieces of copper, one for each of the competing nations.

E A new torch is designed for every relay. Some have been produced by famous designers, but these have not always been very successful; the torch used in Turin in 2006, for example, was criticised for being too heavy for a runner to carry with ease. Different types of fuel have also been tried over the years. The first torches used a natural fuel, such as plant oil. More recently, fuels containing some of the chemicals used in fireworks, such as strontium, have been used to make a more impressive display. However, these have led to technical difficulties at times, as in Melbourne in 1956. On that occasion, the magnesium used produced an extremely bright flame, but it also gave some severe burns to the person carrying it. Since the 1970s, favoured fuels have generally been safer gases such as propane.

Glossary

cauldron (noun) a large metal container

Exam tip

Sometimes, it is not necessary to know the exact meaning of a word. You can use the *context*, or words around one you do not know, to work out what it means.

6 Which questions in exercise 4c were the quickest / easiest to answer? Why? Discuss your answers in pairs.

7 Use the context in the passage to work out the definition of these words (A or B).

a) *copper* (section D)
   A a type of sports equipment
   B a type of metal

b) *strontium* (section E)
   A a type of fuel
   B a type of colour

Cities of the future

1a Look at the following possible places for future cities and number them according to how likely you think it is that humans will live there one day. (1= most likely).

    a) under the ground ....

    b) in very tall skyscrapers (more than 100 floors high) ....

    c) on the moon ....

    d on other planets in our solar system ....

    e) at the bottom of the sea ....

    f) on the sea on artificial islands ....

1b Work in pairs to compare your ideas. Can you think of any other possibilities?

> **Glossary**
>
> *A salt-tolerant vegetable is one that can grow in salty soil or water.

2a Read the question above the text. Then scan the text and underline the names of the vegetables.

What salt-tolerant vegetable* is currently being developed?

Rising sea levels may well be a problem for food production because if land becomes covered with sea water, the salt can make it unsuitable for growing crops. Research is therefore being carried out in the Netherlands to try to develop crops which can still grow well in salty soil. Experiments have previously been carried out with carrots and one variety of onion. However, the most exciting developments at the moment are the attempts to produce a potato like this, as they are the world's fourth most important crop.

> **Exam tip**
>
> A passage may contain two or more items that could be the right answer to a question. You can check which is correct by noting key words or phrases in the question and then reading the passage again to see if they appear. This can help you to find the correct answer.

2b Look back at the question and underline a key word which changes its whole meaning. Then look at the vegetables you underlined and choose the correct one.

3 Follow the procedure in exercise 2 and answer the questions.

    a) How many years will it take to build the Ocean Spiral?

> The Ocean Spiral is a project proposed by the Japanese company Shimizu to provide homes for people on the ocean. Officials at the company say that it will take about five years to construct and that the technology needed to create living conditions below the surface of the ocean could be available in just 12 years' time.

    b) What will be the main form of transport in CCCC's floating city?

> The building company CCCC hopes to build a floating city off the coast of China. It will include a number of facilities for entertaining visitors, such as museums and a theme park. Residents and visitors will travel around the city principally by submarine, although there may also be roads for electric cars.

4 Read the questions (1–9) and decide what type of word or information you need to look for in the passage.

  1 What institutions have often taken advantage of the absence of laws at sea? ....

  2 What destroyed Werner Stiefel's last attempt at creating an offshore platform? ....

  3 What shape will the area of the Ocean Spiral with the living spaces be? ....

  4 What gas will be produced by the Ocean Spiral's 'earth factory'? ....

  5 What material will be used to construct the Ocean Spiral? ....

  6 What kind of floating construction has CCCC already developed? ....

  7 What will be the main purpose of CCCC's floating city? ....

  8 What will provide the main source of energy in the city? ....

  9 What will be the source of drinking water? ....

Exam tip

When answering short answer questions in the IELTS exam, make sure you do not write more words than the word limit given.

✏ EXAM TASK: Reading (short answer questions)

5 **Scan the passage and answer the questions in exercise 4. Choose no more than TWO words or a word and a number from the passage for each answer.**

Floating cities

The oceans cover 71 per cent of the surface of our planet, while humans live on the remaining 29 per cent. But is this a real limit in the modern world or are we coming close to building new cities on the ocean, or even under it?

In the past, plans to establish human settlements on the ocean were often driven by dreams of creating a new society. This is because, beyond an area of 200 nautical miles surrounding any country, there are no laws at sea. In the past, several radio stations have placed themselves at sea to avoid a country's rules about broadcasting. But there have been more ambitious projects too. In the 1960s, the US businessman Werner Stiefel made several attempts to set up a new society called 'Operation Atlantis' in the sea around the Caribbean. None of his projects were successful, and he gave up the idea after a platform that he was building off Cuba broke up in a storm.

In the 21st century, developments in technology and the need to create space for a growing population have made projects for living on the ocean both more realistic and more necessary. One such project is the Ocean Spiral, proposed by the Japanese engineering firm Shimizu.

According to the design, part of this will be a large spherical structure about 500 metres across. This section will provide homes for about 3,000 people. Most of the time it will sit on the surface of the ocean like a floating ball, but it can be pulled down under the water in bad weather. Below this section, a spiral-shaped path will lead to the ocean floor. Here an 'earth factory' will use micro-organisms to turn carbon dioxide into methane. This can be used to generate electricity. The original plan was to use concrete as the main construction material, but Shimizu now plans to build all of the structure from resin*.

Japan is not the only country with plans like this. As China is faced with a need to provide housing for its increasing population, it may also start building cities out in the ocean. The Chinese company CCCC hopes to build a new floating city off the country's coast. The company has already created bridges which can float on water. According to the plan, this technology could form the basis for a complete new city. It will provide living space for some of the residents of China's crowded cities, but the designers see its primary purpose as a tourist attraction. The city is expected to be able to provide its own energy and food. Energy will be mostly provided by the movement of the waves, while the processing of rubbish will provide a secondary source of power. Farms located around the edge of the construction will supply food, and drinking water will be collected from rain and stored in a large freshwater lake.

Shimizu and CCCC's proposed floating cities may seem very ambitious, but both companies insist that they will go ahead.

Glossary

*resin (noun) a solid synthetic material used as the basis of plastic

6 **Scan the passage to find a verb that commonly goes in front of the following nouns:**

a) _establish_ a settlement

b) .... the idea

c) .... electricity

d) .... housing

e) .... the basis for something

f) .... food

7 **Use the verb–noun collocations from exercise 6 to complete the following sentences. Change the tense of the verb if necessary.**

a) His ideas _formed the basis_ for a new social movement and eventually a new political party.

b) If the desert continues to expand, then there will be less land to .... for the hungry population.

c) The minister revealed a programme to .... for the newly arrived refugees in the city.

d) The French successfully ...., which later became the city of Quebec.

e) It is important that humans do not .... of creating a better society.

f) During certain hours, the water from the river flows to a power plant to ....

Diamonds are forever

1a Read the statements about diamonds (a–d) and decide if they are true or false.

a) Diamonds are always transparent with no colour. **T /** **F**

b) A diamond can only be cut by another diamond. **T / F**

c) Diamonds cannot be produced artificially. **T / F**

d) The Ancient Greeks thought that diamonds were pieces of fallen stars. **T / F**

1b Work in pairs to discuss your answers. Then check the answer key. Were there any answers which surprised you?

2a Scan the passage and underline the following words. Do not read the whole passage.

> 'Mountain of Light'   movie   parents   Queen Victoria   2014

2b Which were the easiest words to see? Why? Compare your ideas with a partner.

> **Exam tip**
>
> Scanning is an important skill to practise for the IELTS exam, as it can help you find information quickly. The best words to scan for are ones you know will be in the passage, such as a name or a date.

3 Sometimes the idea in a question is expressed in the passage in different words. Scan the passage and underline the following ideas.

a) the same family still owns it
It is still owned by the same family
(change from active to passive).

b) one of the most uncommon colours

c) larger than any other clear diamond

d) not knowing how valuable the stone was

e) prospectors discovered diamonds in Brazil

> **Exam tip**
>
> When an idea is expressed differently in the passage from the questions, the change can be in the vocabulary (e.g. *not knowing = unaware*), or it can be in the grammar (e.g. *prospectors discovered diamonds in Brazil = diamonds were discovered in Brazil by prospectors*).

4 Scan the passage and underline the diamonds in the box. Look for the capital letters in the names to help you.

A the Koh-i-Noor	**D** the Akbar Shah
B the Daria-i-Noor	**E** the Great Star of Africa
C the Regent diamond	

> **Exam tip**
>
> In a matching question of this type, the items to be matched will normally be listed in the same order as they appear in the passage.

5a Read the statements (1–6). Match the underlined words and phrases with one from the box.

1 _E_ Its current location is <u>uncertain</u>.   *the Akbar Shah*

2 ...... It was frequently worn by a British <u>monarch</u>. ....

3 ...... It was originally <u>part of a larger diamond</u>. ....

4 ...... It has been claimed to be the <u>most beautiful</u> diamond in the world. ....

5 ...... It was lost and then <u>renamed</u>. ....

6 ...... It may have been the inspiration for a famous <u>fictional diamond</u>. ....

> **A** king or queen   **B** given another name   **C** a diamond in a book or film
> **D** cut from a bigger diamond   **E** not known   **F** most spectacular

✎ **EXAM TASK: Reading (matching information)**

5b Read the passage again and match the diamonds in exercise 4 with the statements in exercise 5a. You can use any diamond more than once.

Diamonds are forever

A The world's love of diamonds began in India, where these beautiful stones were found in the country's riverbeds. We do not know when the diamond trade began, but an account book from the 4th century BC shows that they were already being bought and sold by rich Indians at that time. Today the world's diamond trade is centred in Africa, but at its peak the Indian diamond business produced some of the finest stones in the world. One of the most famous is the Koh-i-Noor (Persian for 'Mountain of Light'), which was probably found in the 13th century. First owned by a number of Indian kings, it was then removed when Persians invaded Delhi in 1739 and given a Persian name. Eventually it was returned to India, but as the country was then under British rule it was presented to Queen Victoria, who regularly wore it on a brooch. Later it was set on a crown and became part of the Crown Jewels, where it can still be seen today. A diamond with a similar name, the Daria-i-Noor ('Sea of Light'), is also from India. It is pink in colour, one of the rarest shades of diamond. This is probably the stone which inspired the idea of the Pink Panther diamond in the famous movie of the 1960s. Today it is part of the Iranian Crown Jewels. India is also the origin of what is sometimes said to be the most stunning diamond in existence. This is the Regent diamond, which has a near-perfect cut and is unusually bright. This is now in the Louvre in Paris.

B Because the past of such valuable objects often involves theft and secret deals, large parts of their history are often mysterious. The Akbar Shah, another Indian diamond, disappeared from that country and later reappeared in Turkey with the new name of the 'Shepherd's Stone'. It was last recorded as belonging to the ruler of Baroda in India, but it is unclear whether it is still owned by that same family or has been sold on. Stories about a diamond's history are quite frequently started by diamond dealers to make the stones seem more exotic.

C In the early 1700s, the first diamonds were discovered in Brazil by prospectors* who were actually searching for gold. This began a hunt for further diamonds, which met with success in several parts of the country. Over the centuries Brazil has produced a number of famous diamonds. It remained the world's most important diamond-dealing country until the spectacular discoveries made in South Africa in the 19th century.

D The story of how the South African diamond trade began seems like a fairy tale. Some children playing in a river found a shiny stone, which they took home to their parents. Unaware of its value, they gave it to a travelling salesman who then sold it for a very small sum of money. However, it eventually fell into the hands of an expert who correctly identified it, and so started a diamond boom. South African diamond mines have produced stones of a greater size and quality than any found before. The Blue Moon of Josephine, discovered in South Africa in 2014, fetched the highest price at auction of any jewel. Another notable South African diamond was the Cullinan diamond, which has now been cut into several different stones. One of these is the Great Star of Africa, which is still the largest clear diamond in the world.

Glossary

*prospector (noun) someone who looks for something valuable like gold or oil

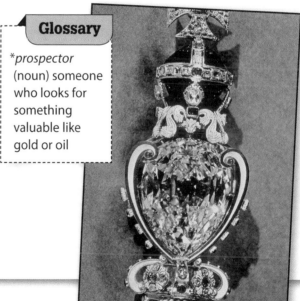

6 **Find words in the passage with the following meanings:**

a) the time when something is at its most successful (section A) ....*peak*........

b) an act of stealing (section B) ....

c) unusual and interesting (section B) ....

d) not knowing (section D) ....

e) a period of economic success (section D) ....

f) a type of public sale (section D) ....

Healthy choices

1a Work in groups. Discuss which of the foods in the box you enjoy eating. Do you have any other favourite snacks?

> cakes   cereal bars   chocolate   crisps   fruit   ice cream   nuts   smoothies

1b Which of these snack foods do you think are healthy or unhealthy?

2 Look at the headings and the pictures in the passage below. Which of the five health mistakes are connected to:

a) Food _1_   **b)** Technology ....   **c)** Body position ....

How healthy are you?

Everyone knows the basics – apples are better for you than doughnuts, and exercise is something you should do. But the media is full of conflicting advice and sometimes the right health choices aren't as obvious. This article explores some common misconceptions* and highlights some potentially unhealthy behaviours.

> **Glossary**
>
> *misconception* (noun) an incorrect understanding of something
> *ripple effect* (noun) when one action affects another, then this in turn affects something else

Health mistake 1: distracted eating

It may seem that watching TV is a good way to relax with a snack at the end of the day. The problem is, a person's hand reaches the bottom of the crisp packet faster when they're multitasking. Instead of stopping when they're full, distracted eaters rely on external cues, like the end of a TV programme, to stop eating, says eating behaviour expert Brian Wansink. He recommends people measure out a single serving of a snack before sitting down, and before they go back for more they should pause for a break, as it can take the stomach up to 20 minutes to signal to the brain that it's full.

Health mistake 2: 'healthy' foods that aren't

Many of the apparently 'healthy' snack choices available to buy are actually loaded with sugar, with some cereal bars containing as much sugar as chocolate bars. Sweet foods cause the body to release insulin, a hormone that makes blood sugar drop suddenly, says Jo Bartel, a dietician. When that happens, the hunger returns, energy levels drop and focusing on a task becomes much more difficult. He says that reading labels is the best way to avoid sugar sources that can cause the body's system to crash. For an average person, sugar intake should be a maximum of 20 to 30 grammes a day according to the World Health Organization.

Health mistake 3: poor posture

When a student is deep in thought in class or an employee is concentrating on their computer screen, they probably don't even realise they're tensing their shoulders and leaning over their desk. But according to Dr Julianna Van der Pluym, poor posture can contribute to headaches and other health issues. What's more, slouching may be linked to increased stress levels. A study from Harvard University found that those who adopt a more healthy posture – relaxed shoulders and straight backs – have lower levels of cortisol, the stress hormone. Experts advise that people working at a desk regularly check their posture by imagining there's a string attached to the top of their head, pulling them up.

Health mistake 4: mobiles at bedtime

It may have become the norm for many to relax with a few games on their phone last thing at night, but research has found that having a mobile phone in the bedroom is the main cause of sleep problems amongst young people. A mobile phone gives out something called blue light, which triggers the brain's 'on' switch, setting off a ripple effect*. The best way to wake up feeling ready for the day is to put mobile devices in another room overnight, says Dr Craig Canapari, director of the Yale Sleep Centre.

Health mistake 5: staring at your computer

One of the most common causes of headaches is hours spent online looking at text on screens. The muscles in the eyes can get stuck constantly firing when someone performs close-up tasks over an extended period of time, explains Dr Douglas Lazzaro, an ophthalmologist. And, like any muscles, they get tired and sore. That's when people may experience the symptoms of digital eyestrain – dry, irritated eyes, blurred vision, and head, neck and back pain. If someone is unable to see a website without putting their face close to the screen, Dr Lazzaro suggests that they visit the optician to get their vision checked.

3 Read the passage and work in groups to discuss the questions.

a) Do you sometimes make any of these health mistakes?

b) Do you agree with the advice?

4a The passage contains advice and opinions from experts. Read the passage again and underline the names of the experts mentioned.

Exam tip

To match people to opinions, scan the passage for the names of people mentioned. Also look for words that describe groups (experts, doctors) or organisations (the World Health Organization).

4b Match the people in exercise 4a to their jobs.

a) an ophthalmologist (a doctor who is an expert in eye problems)   *Dr Douglas Lazzaro*

b) a dietician (someone who gives advice about what people eat)   ....

c) an expert in posture (how people position and move their body)   ....

d) a sleep expert   ....

e) an eating behaviour expert   ....

5a Work in pairs to match the sentence beginnings (1–7) and endings (A–G).

1 Eating behaviour experts <u>say that</u> people who miss breakfast …   *C*

2 Recent research found that people who sleep at least eight hours a night …   ....

3 Experts explain that taking deep breaths …   ....

4 Doctors recommend that you drink at least eight glasses of water a day …   ....

5 Dieticians advise people to eat balanced meals …   ....

6 According to the WHO, millions of young adults are at risk of …   ....

7 Doctors suggest that headphones …   ....

A feeds oxygen to your brain and helps you relax.

B to help you stay focused.

C often find it more difficult to concentrate.

D that contain a mix of fibre, protein and fat.

E that sit on your ears are better than those that fit inside your ears.

F feel less stressed.

G hearing loss from listening to loud music.

Exam tip

Look out for reporting verbs (say, explain, suggest) and other reporting expressions (according to) to identify claims and opinions in a passage.

5b Underline the words or phrases in the statements above that are used to express claims or opinions.

✎ EXAM TASK: Reading (matching information)

6 Look at the following statements of views expressed in the reading passage (1–6) and the list of people below. Match each statement with the correct person (A–F).

1 People eat more when they are focusing on other things.   *C*

2 People should check how much sugar is in the foods they eat.   ....

3 Sitting incorrectly is one factor that can lead to headaches.   ....

4 People who sit in an upright position are less likely to feel stressed.   ....

5 To avoid sleep problems, people should not keep their mobile phone by their bed.   ....

6 Someone may need an eye test if they have to sit close to a computer screen to read.   ....

A Dr Douglas Lazzaro

B Researchers from Harvard University

C Brian Wansink

D Dr Craig Canapari

E Dr Julianna Van der Pluym

F Jo Bartel

Mapping the world

1 Work in groups. What type of maps do you use? How and when do you use them?

2 Read the paragraph from a short article from 2013. Answer the questions in pairs.

a) Where did the Google team go?

b) Why did they go?

c) What will Google Maps users be able to see?

d) What is the Trekker backpack?

Soon you won't have to travel all the way to Arizona to see the Grand Canyon. A team from Google has hiked miles of the canyon's trails. Along the way, they recorded views of the giant gorge using Trekker backpacks (fitted with smaller versions of Google's StreetView camera). They descended through thousands of feet of rock which was worn away over millions of years by the Colorado River. The views will be available this year for anyone to see on Google Maps.

3a Summarise the paragraph with your partner.

3b Read the headings. Which one best describes the main idea in the paragraph in exercise 2? Why are the other headings not appropriate?

1 A global collection of online maps

2 A project to photograph the Grand Canyon

3 The formation process that created the Grand Canyon

4a Read the longer passage from 2015 about the same topic. Underline the places it mentions that Google Maps has photographed.

4b Work in groups and answer the questions.

a) What type of camera did they use to photograph each of the places mentioned?

b) Why did they need special cameras for some of the places?

c) Is the article mainly about the different places that the Google team has visited or about the types of cameras they used?

4c Which of the places mentioned in the text would you like to see?

5 Match the general words and phrases in the box to extracts from the passage.

> the background   a context   a design solution   ~~a particular location~~

a) the Liwa Oasis in the United Arab Emirates   *a particular location*

b) The Street View project started off … and then … ....

c) We needed them to work in the desert and the Arctic … so they designed the Trekker camera system to withstand extreme cold and blazing heat

....

d) narrow lanes and alleyways in cities ....

Exam tip

Headings often summarise the main idea in a section using a more general word.

6a Read the headings in the task below and underline the general words and phrases.

Exam tip

Exam questions sometimes use Roman numerals – i, ii, iii, iv, v, etc. Make sure you are familiar with the Roman numerals for the numbers 1 to 10.

✎ EXAM TASK: Reading (matching headings)

6b The passage has five sections, A–E. Choose the correct heading for sections A–E from the list of headings below. Write the correct number, i–vii.

   i Applications of the technology for other projects

   ii The background to the project

   iii The results for the end user

   iv An approach to a task in a particular location

   v The importance of an adaptable design solution

   vi The future goals of the project

   vii Adaptations of the technology for different contexts

Camel Cam

A ....

Over three days last June, a camel carried a special camera across the Liwa Oasis in the United Arab Emirates. A team of Google employees walked alongside the camel and its handler for three hours each day while the camera took pictures. The hike was part of Google's mission to capture images for its Street View project.

B ....

Google has been collecting photos all over the world since 2007. When you visit Google Maps, you can see what it would look like to stand in a particular spot. The Street View project started off taking photos in a handful of US cities and then expanded globally. So far, you can see Street View pictures from 63 countries, including Bhutan.

C ....

Usually, cars drive around equipped with Street View cameras. But what about the places where cars can't go? That's where the Trekker comes in. It's a slimmed-down version that can be carried in a large backpack. Like the original Street View camera, the Trekker system has 50 cameras arranged to get a 360-degree panoramic view. Each camera takes a picture every 2.5 seconds. After Google collects the pictures, it uses a computer program to put them together to make a single image that you can view online.

Google built its cameras so they can travel anywhere. 'We needed them to work in the desert and the Arctic,' says Steve Silverman, a Google engineer. So they designed the Trekker camera system to cope with extreme cold and blazing heat, from -26 to 46 degrees Celsius. It even works underwater.

D ....

As well as the Trekker system, Google has adapted its cameras for a variety of different conditions and terrain. The Street View Trike was designed to fit down narrow streets which are inaccessible by car. The camera is mounted on the back of a tricycle – a three-wheeled bike – which automatically gathers images as the operator cycles around. The Trike has been used to capture images in the narrow lanes and alleyways of cities like Barcelona and Paris.

To offer users an inside view of public buildings, Street View has also gone indoors to explore museums, sports stadiums and even the White House. To fit through narrow doorways and navigate* around objects, Google fitted all the necessary equipment onto a narrow cart on wheels known as the Street View Trolley.

E ....

Why go to such efforts? Not everyone can visit these sites in person. Thanks to the Trekker, anyone can tour the Grand Canyon, the frozen Arctic or the pyramids in Egypt – all without leaving home.

Glossary

navigate (verb) to move or travel around a place

7 Put the words from the passage into five groups according to their meaning.

> capture gather image indoors photograph picture site spot

Exam tip

Notice synonyms (words with a similar meaning) in a reading passage. Often a writer uses synonyms to avoid repeating the same word.

Nouns	Nouns	Verbs	Verbs	Adverbs
a photo	a place	to take (a photo)	to collect (pictures)	inside
a [a]*picture*	a [c]...........	to [e]........... (a photo)	to [g]........... (pictures)	[h]...........
an [b]...........	a [d]...........	to [f]........... (a place)		

Connections

1 **Work in groups. Look at the infographic and answer the questions.**

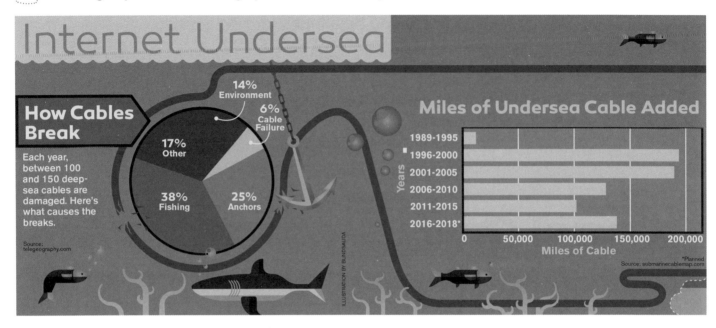

a) During which period was the largest amount of internet cable laid under the sea? Why do you think that was?

b) What is the most common cause of damage to undersea internet cables? What do you think happens to them?

2a **Work in pairs. Read the definition of the word infrastructure. Think of more examples of transport infrastructure.**

infrastructure (noun) [U] the basic equipment and services needed for a large system to run smoothly, such as a communications system or the energy system in a country

Transport infrastructure: roads, railway stations …

2b **Read section A of the passage and discuss the questions.**

a) What types of internet infrastructure are mentioned?

b) What is the main topic of this section? Think of a possible heading for it.

3 **Read the complete passage and find examples of these things:**

a) things that can damage internet infrastructure   **A** on land   **B** under the sea

b) a new cable that may be installed

c) how a new internet cable could improve communication

Exam tip

It is sometimes possible to guess the meaning of unknown words using information in the text around them.

4 **Find these words in the passage. Identify the part of speech (noun, verb, adjective). What do you think the word means? What helped you guess the meaning?**

a) Section B: criss-cross *(verb)*

b) Section C: invincible (...........)

c) Section C: vulnerable (...........)

d) Section D: prone to (...........)

e) Section D: obstacles (...........)

f) Section E: passageway (...........)

Exam tip

To identify the topic of each section you need to look at the first sentence (general idea) and the second sentence (specific detail) together.'

5 **Work in pairs. Look at the first two sentences of these paragraphs. What general idea does the first sentence express? Which more specific detail does the second sentence describe?**

1 Section C   **2** Section D   **3** Section E, paragraph 1

Connecting the globe

A ....

We all use the internet all the time. But what is the internet actually made of? And when you type a password into a login screen or enter a search term into Google, where does it go?

The internet is a global network that allows us to connect with people anywhere. But it couldn't exist without the vast web of mobile phone towers, cables and other structures that keep our vital communications running. Some of these components are underwater or underground, while others are in buildings. 'The internet sometimes seems very abstract, but it depends on physical infrastructure to work,' says Paul Brodsky, an analyst at a telecommunications research company. 'It's an amazing combination of civil, electrical, marine and computer engineering.'

B ....

Every year, Brodsky and his colleagues produce a global map of the undersea cables that allow for high-speed communications across the world's oceans. 'Over 99 per cent of long-distance communications today – web data, online videos and even phone calls – travel through fibre optic cables,' says Brodsky.

Each fibre optic cable contains very thin strands* of glass. Data is converted into pulses of light that travel at incredible speed through the glass. Millions of kilometres of fibre optic cable criss-cross the world, allowing for high-speed data transfer.

C ....

Internet infrastructure keeps our communications flowing, but it isn't invincible. It's vulnerable to threats like natural disasters. Hurricane Katrina, in the USA in 2005, knocked down mobile phone towers and flooded power stations, causing widespread communication problems. To keep connections working, says computer scientist Paul Barford, 'you want to have different ways of getting from A to B, so that if one path is blocked, you have an alternative.'

D ....

New connections are being added all the time, both on land and at sea. Installing a cable at sea is a massive task. It requires finding the safest possible route along the sea floor, avoiding areas prone to earthquakes or containing fragile coral reefs. Surveyors also look out for obstacles, such as sunken ships, that could break the cable. In shallow waters, anchors and fishermen's nets can cut cables, so the lines are buried an average of two metres below the sea floor. In the deep sea, where there's less activity, the cables sit right on top of the seabed. There are areas where it's previously been impossible to lay cables – like across the Arctic Ocean, which is usually covered with ice for much of the year.

E ....

One project aims to take advantage of climate change. Melting sea ice in the Arctic has opened up a new passageway between Asia and Europe. One company has proposed laying a new cable that would link Tokyo, Japan, and London, England, cutting a huge amount of time from communication between these two global financial centres. Data would be able to travel one way in just 154 milliseconds, instead of 178 milliseconds as it does now. It would also deliver the first fibre optic internet connections to communities in Alaska and northern Canada.

✎ EXAM TASK: Reading (matching headings)

6 The passage has five sections, A–E. Choose the correct heading for sections A–E from the list of headings below. Write the correct number, i–viii.

- **i** New connections to improve global communication
- **ii** A network of cables
- **iii** Internet infrastructure
- **iv** The impact of climate change on internet infrastructure
- **v** The challenges of laying undersea cables
- **vi** The increasing role of the internet in global business
- **vii** Threats to internet infrastructure
- **viii** The impact of internet cables on the fishing industry

> **Exam tip**
>
> For this task, the passage will be divided into sections. Each section may be one paragraph or it may be two or three paragraphs. You need to find a heading that describes the whole section if there is more than one paragraph in it.

Survival is in the eyes

1 Work in groups. Describe the animals in the pictures. Use the questions and the words in the box to help you.

a) What do they look like?

b) Do they hunt other animals or are they hunted themselves?

c) How is their body adapted to the way they live?

> antlers   catch   ears   escape   eyesight
> fur   graze   hearing   hunt   mane   tail

2a You are going to read a passage about the eyes of animals. Scan the passage for the names of different animals and underline them.

2b Divide the animals in the passage into two groups: A predators (hunters) and B prey (animals that are hunted).

3a Work in groups of four. Two students in each group are A, two students are B.

A students: Scan the passage for information about predators. Read these sections again carefully and answer the questions. a) What shape are the pupils of predators? b) How does this help them to hunt?	**B students:** Scan the passage for information about prey animals. Read these sections again carefully and answer the questions. a) What shape are the pupils of prey animals? b) How does this help them avoid predators?

3b Share your answers and compare the differences between the two groups of animals.

4 Which sections of the passage are mainly about predators and which are mainly about prey animals? Which sections are about both, or something different?

> **Exam tip**
>
> If there are two (or more) key topics in a passage, such as different places, different groups of people or different types of animals, note down which sections are about which topic. This will help you to match the headings to the correct sections.

5 Find a word or phrase in the passage with a similar meaning.

a) (section A) variation *differences*

b) (section A) eyesight ....

c) (section B) hunters ....

d) (section C) modelled ....

e) (section E) possible ....

> **Exam tip**
>
> It is a good idea to scan for key words that are the same as those in a heading, and also for words with a similar meaning, because headings often contain a synonym of a key word in the section.

6a Work in pairs. Look at these possible headings for section A and underline the key words in each one. Are the same key words in the section? Can you find words with a similar meaning in the section?

1 A comparison between human and animal pupil shape

2 A question about the reasons behind variation in pupil shape

3 Research into how different animals' pupils vary in shape

6b Read the section again. Which heading best matches the main idea in the section? Why are the other headings less appropriate?

PHOTOCOPIABLE

A ....

Look into the eyes of a person and you'll notice the dark, circular pupil in the centre of each one. This opening allows light into the eyes so we can see. Look into the eyes of another species, however, and you may notice some major differences in pupil shapes. For example, cats' pupils can narrow into thin vertical slits and goats' pupils look like horizontal lines.

Vision scientist Martin Banks of the University of California and his colleagues wanted to investigate the reasons behind these differences: Why do different pupil shapes exist, and why does a particular species have one shape instead of another?

B ....

To learn more about animals' eyes, Banks and his team collected photos and descriptions of the eyes of 214 land animals. They also classified what kind of lifestyle each creature had: whether it was a predator (an animal that hunts and eats other animals) or prey (one that gets eaten).

They found that the shape of an animal's pupil depends on its role in an ecosystem. 'Vertical slit pupils occur in predators,' says Banks. 'Most are ambush predators, which means they wait for their prey to get close and then pounce* on it.'

C ....

The team wanted to understand how vertical pupils might help these pouncing predators. To investigate, they simulated the pupil of an eye using a camera's aperture, the opening that lets in light. The scientists adjusted the aperture into a vertical slit and took photos.

When a camera – or eye – focuses on something close to it, other objects slightly nearer or farther away appear a little blurry, or unclear. You can see this by closing one eye, holding two fingers at different distances from your face and focusing on one finger and then the other. This effect, called blur, helps a viewer estimate the distance to a nearby object.

D ....

Banks and his colleagues found that a vertical slit aperture enhances the effect of blur. In the case of an animal's eye, that means vertical pupils probably help cats or other predators determine exactly how far away their prey is, so they can pounce just the right distance.

Banks's team also noticed that animals with vertical pupils usually have eyes on the front of their face rather than on the sides of their head. This allows predators to focus both eyes on a single object, an ability called 'binocular vision'. Each eye sees a slightly different image and the brain combines the two of them to create the perception of depth. Like blur, binocular vision helps viewers judge the distance to an object and it's even more powerful in vertical pupils.

E ....

Unlike predators, prey animals such as sheep, goats, deer and horses have eyes on the sides of their heads and horizontal pupils. These features maximise the animals' field of view, the area they can see around themselves. The animals don't know what direction a potential predator might come from, 'So they have to watch all around: in front, to the sides and behind,' says Banks. Once an animal spots a predator, it needs to run away. Horizontal pupils give animals with eyes on the sides of their head a much better view to the front than other shapes would.

Glossary

pounce (verb) to jump on something, especially to catch it

✏ EXAM TASK: Reading (matching headings)

7 **Choose the correct heading for sections B–F from the list of headings below.**

 i An experiment to model the effects of a vertical pupil ....

 ii An explanation of why predators have better eyesight than their prey ....

 iii Two reasons why pupil shape may help avoid possible threats ....

 iv A question about the reasons behind variation in pupil shape ...A...

 v An outline of a research project into pupil shape ....

 vi Two different pupil shapes which help animals escape predators ....

 vii How certain pupil shapes may be better suited to hunting ....

Endangered and extinct

1 **Work in pairs. Discuss the following questions.**
Use the pictures and prompts to help you.

  1 Which of the following animals are in danger of extinction
  (= when all the animals of a species have died)?

  2 What are the reasons why some of these animals are endangered?

  > crocodiles   elephants   kangaroos   pandas   rhinos   tigers

  - hunting
  - habitat loss (e.g. cutting down forests)
  - pollution
  - disease

2 **Skim the reading passage quickly. In groups, discuss the questions.**

  a) What type of animal is the passage about?

  b) Where did it live?

  c) Why did it become extinct?

  d) When did the last animal die?

  e) How are pigeons viewed in your culture; are they kept as pets or are they hunted?

3 **Find words in the passage from the same word family.**

  a) destroy (verb)   *destructive* (adjective)

  b) arrive (verb)   .... (noun)

  c) commercial (adjective)   .... (verb)

  d) construct (verb)   .... (noun)

  e) invent (verb)   .... (noun)

  f) move (verb)   .... (noun)

  g) lose (verb)   .... (noun)

  h) disappear (verb)   .... (noun)

4a **Match the general phrases with the specific examples in the box.**
Write the correct letter.

  a) Technological developments   ....

  b) Restrictions on hunting   ....

  c) Changes to the landscape   ....

  d) An American state   ....

  > **A** ban on shooting   **B** cutting down forests   **C** the telephone
  > **D** building roads   **E** California   **F** no trapping   **G** Texas   **H** aeroplanes

> **Exam tip**
>
> In this type of exam task, the question often describes a general idea, e.g. damage to farmland, which matches more specific examples in the passage, e.g. crops eaten, trees fallen.

4b **Think of some other specific examples that could be matched with a–d.**
Work in pairs to compare your ideas.

5a **Read the statements, 1–6. Underline the key words that describe a general idea.**

  1 Technological developments that speeded the pigeons' extinction ....

  2 A reason why passenger pigeons were easy for hunters to kill ....

  3 Details of the damage passenger pigeons could do to farmland ....

  4 How colonisation changed the landscape of one American state ....

  5 Details of legal restrictions on hunting ....

  6 A reason why the arrival of the pigeons may have been welcomed ....

✏ **EXAM TASK: Reading (Matching features)**

5b Read paragraph A of the passage again. Choose TWO statements in exercise 5a which match the information in the paragraph.

6 Now reread the rest of the passage and match the statements in exercise 5a to the correct paragraph, A–E.

Exam tip

In a set of 'Matching features' questions, one paragraph may contain two or even more of the items. There may also be some paragraphs that you do not use at all.

Exam tip

For this type of question, read the questions first. Then read the whole passage, one section at a time. Stop after each one so that you answer the questions as you go through.

The loss of the passenger pigeon

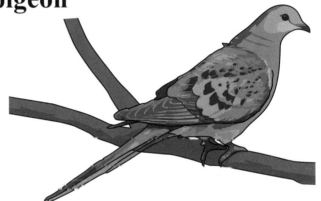

A Passenger pigeons were once the most common bird in North America and, perhaps, the world. They travelled in groups so large that they often darkened the sky. Visitors to the USA and Canada were amazed at their numbers. No doubt the sight of a flock, or group, could be good news at certain times of the year, as their meat was a good source of food. But the pigeons were also very destructive. Farmers could find their crops eaten and trees fallen under the weight of the masses of birds.

B It seems incredible that a bird which once existed in such numbers could vanish in just over a century. Yet by October 1914, the passenger pigeon was extinct, a victim of the uncontrolled activity of professional hunters. Of course, even before the arrival of Europeans, Native Americans had trapped and killed them for food. What caused their extinction was the fact that hunting became commercialised. In the mid-19th century, the construction of national railways and the invention of the telegraph made it possible for pigeon hunting to develop hugely in the USA. Professional hunters could track their movements around the North American continent and the birds were shot or caught in nets in huge numbers.

C Loss of habitat was another factor. The pigeons fed on the nuts of the oak and beech trees that covered large parts of North America. Before the Europeans arrived, Ohio, for example, was almost completely covered in forest. However, by the early 20th century around 90 per cent of these trees had been cut down.

D It was the pigeons' habit of gathering in enormous flocks and nesting in large groups that made them vulnerable to extinction. A species of animal concentrated in one space can be shot and killed in large numbers very easily. Passenger pigeons were a highly social species and could only breed when they lived in large groups. When they were reduced to living in much smaller groups, their fertility* declined and they did not raise chicks.

E In the later part of the 19th century, some efforts were made to stop the killing of pigeons. In the state of Michigan, for example, a ban was placed on shooting or trapping pigeons within two miles of their nesting areas. Ultimately, though, this was too late to save the species. As numbers continued to decline, a number of attempts were made to breed the birds. In 1902, a female bird named Martha was sent to Cincinnati Zoo, where it was hoped that she would raise young. Unfortunately, this never happened. In 1907, following the death of four males in captivity in Wisconsin, Martha and her two male companions were the last surviving pigeons in the world. The disappearance of the species from the planet can be given to the hour: Martha died at 1 pm on 1 September 1914, still in her cage at the zoo.

Glossary

*fertility (noun) the ability of an animal to have babies

Firestorm

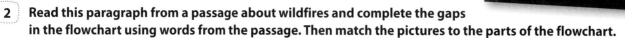

1 Work in groups. Which of these factors do you think cause wildfires? Explain why.

> campfires   dropped cigarettes   dry wood   hot weather   lightning   rain   wind

2 Read this paragraph from a passage about wildfires and complete the gaps in the flowchart using words from the passage. Then match the pictures to the parts of the flowchart.

a    b    c

> Wildfires happen when three factors come together, says Matt Jolly, an ecologist from the US Forest Service. The first factor is the weather. Hot, dry and windy conditions dry out branches and other dead plant material on the forest floor. This material becomes the second factor: fuel. Once weather conditions and fuel are in place, all that's needed is a source of ignition: something that starts the fire. In the western USA that is usually lightning, says Jolly. In the eastern USA, fires are often started by human activity, sometimes by accident – for example, when a campfire isn't put out properly.

| **Factor 1:** hot, dry, windy weather conditions *Picture C* | | **Factor 2:** dry branches and other plant material become .... | | **Factor 3:** a source of ...., such as lightning |

3 Which of these pieces of information does the paragraph contain?

a) The main factors which lead to wildfires

b) Statistics about wildfire trends globally

c) The role of the weather in causing wildfires

d) The effects of wildfires on people

4a Complete the definitions with the words from the box.

> cause   effect   factor   risk

a) .... : one of several things that influences what happens

b) .... : the possibility that something bad might happen

c) .... : the reason why something happens

d) .... : a change that happens because of something

4b Now read the full passage. Work in pairs to find the following information.

a) Paragraphs A and B: Find two effects of the wildfires in the USA in 2015.

b) Paragraph C: Find two causes of wildfires in the USA; one natural and one human.

c) Paragraph D: Find one positive effect of natural wildfires.

d) Paragraph E: Find which area of the world is most at risk of wildfires.

e) Paragraph F: Find four factors which scientists believe increase the risk of wildfires.

> **Exam tip**
>
> Look out for key words in a passage which tell you how ideas are linked together, such as risk factor, cause and effect. Remember that *risk* and *cause* can be used as nouns or verbs: *He risked his life to save her. The fires caused huge damage.* But *effect* is always a noun – the verb form is *affect*: *Thousands of people were affected by the fires.*

5a Underline the key nouns in the questions, 1–6, below. Look for sentences in the passage that express the same idea.

🖉 **EXAM TASK: Reading (Matching features)**

5b Which paragraphs contain the following information? Write the correct letter, A–I. You may use the same letter more than once.

1 The trend for more severe fire seasons in the USA _B_

2 The positive effect of wildfires on the forest ecosystem ....

3 The results of research into global wildfire trends ....

4 The most common ways that wildfires are ignited in the USA ....

5 A description of research into wildfire trends ....

Firestorm

A During a single weekend in June 2015, 152 wildfires started in Alaska, the most northerly state in the USA. Flames spread through fallen branches which had been dried out by warm conditions and turned into perfect fuel. In total, more than 5 million acres of Alaskan forests burned.

B Alaska wasn't the only US state on fire, as blazes raged across California, Washington and much of the western USA. Thousands of people were evacuated as flames threatened homes. Extreme fire seasons like this are becoming more common. Before 2000, more than 8 million acres had never burned in one year in the USA. Since 2000, there have been six years when that has happened. Some believe this trend could be the new normal.

C Wildfires happen when three factors come together, says Matt Jolly, an ecologist from the US Forest Service. The first factor is the weather. Hot, dry, and windy conditions dry out branches and other dead plant material on the forest floor. The material becomes the second factor: fuel. Once weather conditions and fuel are in place, all that's needed is a source of ignition: something that starts the fire. In the western USA that is usually lightning says Jolly. In the eastern USA, fires are often started by human activity, sometimes by accident – for example, when a campfire isn't put out properly.

D People tend to view fire as a catastrophe. It's true that human-caused wildfires are never a good idea, but naturally occurring wildfires aren't always a bad thing, Jolly says. Forests rely on fires to stay healthy. Blazes clear the forest floor so that new trees can grow. 'Fire has always been a part of nature,' says Jolly. 'It's when fires threaten people's lives and property that we see them as disasters.'

E There is clearly documented evidence of the increased incidence of wildfires in the USA in recent decades, but it was unclear whether the same picture was being seen globally. Anecdotal evidence* suggests that this is a widespread phenomenon, with more severe wildfires breaking out across the globe. Some 54 per cent of all wildfires occur in Africa, with particular hotspots in Angola and the Democratic Republic of Congo. Some of the most extreme forest fires in recent times have burned across Indonesia, the Philippines and Laos. Until recently, though, there was no comprehensive overview of wildfire trends.

F Jolly and his colleagues studied weather data from around the world that scientists had gathered over the past 35 years. He and his team looked for four factors that increase the chance of wildfires: high temperatures, low humidity*, many rain-free days and high wind speeds. They identified places that had experienced all these conditions at once, and measured how long they had experienced them. That told them how long the fire seasons around the world had been from 1979 to 2013. 'Being able to combine information about each day for every place on the planet was really powerful,' says Jolly.

G Jolly and his team found that across one quarter of the parts of Earth's surface where plants grow, fire season has lengthened. Globally, they found that fire season has become more than 18 per cent longer, from 18 days to 22 days on average. They also found that the total area at risk of fires has doubled, increasing from 11.4 million to 23.5 million square kilometres. 'It's clear that something has changed over the last 35 years,' says Jolly.

H The world is gradually heating up due to the effects of climate change. The Earth's climate has always varied over time, but over the past 100 years average temperatures have risen unusually quickly. Alaska, for example, has warmed by more than 1.7°C in the past 50 years.

Portrait of Venus

1 **Work in pairs. What do you know about the solar system? Answer the questions with a planet from the box. You can use each planet more than once.**

> Earth   Jupiter   Mars   ~~Mercury~~   Neptune   Saturn   Venus

Which planet …

a) is the closest to / the furthest from the Sun?
Mercury / ....

b) is the largest / the smallest / the second smallest?
....

c) is famous for its rings? ....

d) supports life? ....

e) has the hottest surface temperature? ....

2 **Answers to sentence completion questions are usually nouns, but these can be singular, plural or uncountable. What type of noun is needed for the sentences? Choose the correct answer.**

a) Neptune was first seen through a _telescope_ (singular noun) / plural noun) in 1846.

b) Jupiter's atmosphere consists mainly of .... (singular noun / uncountable noun).

c) In 1610, the astronomer Galileo discovered four .... (singular noun / plural noun) circling the planet Jupiter.

d) The red colour of the planet Mars is caused by .... (singular noun / uncountable noun) in its rocks.

e) Neptune is believed to have a rocky .... (singular noun / uncountable noun), approximately the same size as the Earth.

> **Exam tip**
>
> The article before a gap can tell you what kind of word is needed. When there is 'a', it must be a singular countable noun. When there is no article (no 'a' or 'the') before the gap, then the answer must be a plural or an uncountable noun.

3 **Choose the best answer for the sentences in exercise 2 from the words in the box.**

> centre   hydrogen   iron   moons   ~~telescope~~

4 **Read the sentences and look at the verbs in bold. Decide if the gaps need a singular or uncountable noun (A) or a plural noun (B).**

a) The _footprints_ that astronauts made on the first moon landing **are** still there on its surface. A / (B)

b) The largest .... in the solar system **is** found on Mars. A / B

c) It appears that .... frequently **take** place on Mars. A / B

d) The .... of the planet Saturn **were** first observed in 1610. A / B

e) There is evidence that .... on Mars and Venus **has** reshaped the surface of both planets. A / B

> **Exam tip**
>
> The verb after a gap can also tell you what kind of noun to look for. For example, a verb with the third person 's' tells you it must be a singular or uncountable noun.

5 **Choose the best answer for the sentences in exercise 4 from the words in the box. Use the grammatical clues and the sense of the sentence to help you.**

> dust storms   ~~footprints~~   mountain   rings   volcanic activity

6 Read the sentences and underline any names or dates that you can use to scan the main text.
(Do not underline the word *Venus*, as this appears in the text many times.)

1 Venus reaches its maximum ...*brightness*... at the beginning and the end of the day.

2 The claim that Phosphorus and Hesperus were the same object was first made by a ....

3 Galileo discovered that Venus passes through a number of different ....

4 In 1961, the radius of Venus was calculated by using ....

5 Just before the Magellan probe was destroyed, it sent back information about the .... of the atmosphere on Venus.

6 Before the 1960s, it was thought that the Venusian environment might be similar to a ....

7 There are signs that some of the .... on Venus are active today.

8 The clouds on Venus are similar to the clouds on Earth in that they can generate ....

9 It is possible that .... was plentiful on Venus billions of years ago.

✏ EXAM TASK: Reading (sentence completion)

7 Complete the sentences in exercise 6. Choose ONE word to complete each gap. Use the words you underlined to help you.

Exam tip

When answering this type of question, you must use the word as you find it in the text. You CANNOT change it in any way, e.g. by adding an *s*.

Portrait of Venus

A Unlike most of the planets in our solar system, Venus can easily be seen without a telescope. It has therefore long been familiar to humans, although it was often believed to be two separate planets. Its brightness is greatest at sunrise and at sunset, and so the ancient Greeks referred to it both as the morning star (Phosphorus) and the evening star (Hesperus). The first person to decide that these were the same object was the Greek philosopher Pythagoras.

B When Galileo Galilei, the famous Italian astronomer, first pointed a telescope at the planet in the 17th century, he found that it goes through various phases, just as the moon varies from being a full moon to a half moon to a crescent. This discovery was clear evidence that Venus went round the Sun, and it helped to support his general view that planets circled the Sun and not the Earth.

C Apart from this information, Venus remained mysterious until the 20th century. It was only when more advanced methods of investigation became available that more was discovered about it. In 1961, radar signals were used to explore the surface of the planet, allowing astronomers* to make an accurate measurement of its radius. Then the US Magellan probe, launched in 1989, made a map of a large part of the planet's surface. The images that it sent back were like photographs in quality. The final information that the probe gained was a calculation of the atmospheric density. The probe was then destroyed.

D The fact that Venus is a similar size to Earth but closer to the Sun caused some astronomers to think that it might be covered in vegetation, something like a rainforest on Earth.

However, when the investigations began, they showed that the truth was very different. Conditions on Venus are totally unsuited to life, and they have actually been compared to traditional descriptions of Hell.

E Venus has a great many volcanoes – more than any other planet in our solar system – and it has largely been shaped by their eruptions. Astronomers have detected changes in temperature on the surface, which suggests that a number of these are still active. Other forces which can change the shape of our own planet's surface, like wind and rain, have little or no effect on Venus. There is no rainfall and any wind is very light.

F Venus has a very dense atmosphere which is formed mainly of carbon dioxide. Above this layer of gas the planet is covered in clouds, which are mostly sulphuric acid. Just like on Earth, these clouds can produce lightning. This carbon dioxide and thick cloud cover have caused the planet to heat up to a temperature of around 460°C. This makes Venus the hottest of all the planets in the solar system, even though it is not the nearest to the Sun.

G Astronomers have suggested that billions of years ago, Venus may have been much more like Earth. There may even have been large quantities of water on its surface. Somehow, perhaps due to the volcanic activity, temperatures started to rise so that it all evaporated and the current blanket of carbon dioxide was formed. Now that our own planet is faced with global warming, and perhaps permanent climate change, the conditions on our sister planet Venus should serve as a warning to us all.

Glossary

astronomer (noun) a scientist who studies the stars and planets

---

Citrus greening

soya beans

1a   What countries are the world's top producers of the following crops?
Complete the table with the countries from the box.
Then work in pairs to compare your ideas.

Brazil   ~~China~~   Indonesia   Ivory Coast   Spain   USA

tea plant

Crop	Top producer
tea	*China*
olive oil	
cocoa	
soya beans	
coconuts	
oranges	

coconuts

cocoa pod and beans

1b   Work in groups. What are the most important crops in your country? Why?

2   Read the sentences. Put a tick (✓) if the gapfill answer is possible, and a cross (✗) if it repeats information which is already in the sentence.

Exam tip

When completing sentences, you must be sure that the word you write in the gap gives new information and does not repeat an idea which is already in the sentence. Re-read the sentence with your answer to check for this.

a)   When a plant has the disease, its leaves will start to *drop* and eventually they will fall. ✗

b)   Sunlight can be used to kill the *bacteria* that may collect in rainwater. ......

c)   A variety of crops are grown on the farm, but the most important is *sweetcorn* . ...

d)   As the century continued, there was a decline in agriculture and a rise in the importance of *farming* . ...

e)   The increase in the number of farm labourers without work was mainly caused by *unemployment* . ...

f)   The plants form a cover over the lake which blocks sunlight and means that the water lacks *oxygen* . ...

✎ EXAM TASK: Reading (diagram label completion)

3   Read the flow chart below which describes the progress of a disease. Underline a word or phrase in each stage that you can use to scan the text.

| 1 The citrus tree is infected by an insect. | 2 The disease lies inactive for a period in the tree's (a) .... | 3 The bacteria block the tree's food and water system and prevent the movement of (b) .... | 4 The veins in the tree's leaves turn (c) .... | 5 The tree produces (d) .... shaped fruit which has a (e) .... taste. |

4   The stages of a process are often connected with a time word or a result word. Read the words and phrase. Write (A) for a time change and (B) for a result.

then *A*   as a result ......   in consequence ......   after that ......   eventually ......   therefore ......

5   Scan the main passage to find the paragraph which describes the progress of the disease. Then scan this paragraph and underline any time or result words. Then complete the gaps in exercise 3 (2–5). Write ONE word in each gap.

6 **Choose one of the processes in the box. Make some notes on the process. Then work in pairs and describe your process to each other using the time and result words in exercise 4.**

> How a disease or illness develops   How a plant or insect grows   Something from your area of work or study

7 **Complete the sentences. Use ONE word from the passage in each gap.**

1 Placing an infected tree in a heated ___tent___ may help to slow the progress of the disease.

2 Domestic growers of citrus trees are less likely to use _____ than commercial growers.

3 One way of controlling the disease may be to use a kind of _____ which preys on the citrus psyllid.

4 The citrus industry has reallocated some of its _____ budget to fund research into the disease.

5 Spinach genes have been introduced into orange trees as they contain _____ that attack the bacteria.

6 It is hoped that _____ will accept oranges that have been modified by spinach genes.

Citrus greening

A A patient is battling a deadly disease but experts have decided that heat treatment may help. The heat is designed to kill the bacteria that are attacking the victim. Experts hope that it will allow the patient to live a few more years, but there is no cure.

B The patient in question is not a person but a Florida orange tree, and the disease is known as citrus greening. It started in Asia but was accidentally introduced into Florida in 2005. Since then it has spread to most orange-growing regions in the USA and has become a threat to the whole citrus fruit industry.

C The disease is spread by an insect called the citrus psyllid. When the psyllid feeds on an infected tree, it picks up the bacteria and then transports it to another. The signs of the disease may take two to four years to appear. During this time, the disease stays in the roots of the tree. After this, however, it starts to move up the trunk and to multiply in the tree's food and water transport system. This stops the flow of sugars that the tree needs in order to thrive. In consequence, the leaves develop a spotted appearance and their veins start to become yellow. Eventually the leaves fall and whole branches start to die. The fruit on the tree do not become ripe but remain half green, and they are irregular in shape with a very bitter flavour.

D A number of measures have been tried to limit the effects of the disease. The bacteria are heat sensitive, and so moving an infected tree into a plastic tent where a high temperature is maintained can give it a longer life. Eventually, however, the disease takes hold again. Other measures involve targeting the citrus psyllid. Trees can be sprayed with pesticides but these will not stop it completely. This treatment is also expensive, and although the owners of large-scale commercial orchards may be able to afford it, many citrus trees are grown in domestic gardens. It is unlikely that the owners of these spaces will be able to pay for this kind of intensive chemical treatment. Another way of reducing the number of the citrus psyllid may be to use a natural predator. In California experts have tried releasing a species of wasp known to attack the psyllid, with some success. But there is still a need to find a complete solution to the problem. The citrus industry has taken some of the funds that were originally intended for advertising and instead used them for research, in the hope that a real cure can be found.

E Previous experience with similar diseases suggests that the battle against the disease may be won not by trying to cure it, but by developing trees which can resist it. This can be done by using genes from a related species which is not affected by it. In the case of citrus greening, there are no related species that the disease cannot attack, and so researchers have had to turn to unrelated plants. In particular, spinach contains a number of powerful proteins that can target the bacteria which are responsible for the disease. Experiments where these have been introduced into an orange tree appear to have met with success in creating a new, resistant type of tree.

F The biggest problem with this approach may be a commercial one. The spinach proteins have no effect on the taste of the fruit, but will consumers be happy to buy oranges which are grown in this way? Both scientists and growers are hopeful that they can be persuaded, especially if the alternative is the end of the whole citrus fruit industry.

People of the Tenere Desert

1a Look at the places below. What kind of lifestyle do you think people who traditionally live there have? Think about:

- types of houses
- traditional sources of food
- common plants grown or animals kept
- traditional skills

1b Work in pairs to compare your ideas.

2 You are going to read a passage about people living in the Tenere desert. Skim the text and tick (✓) the ideas which are mentioned. Note the paragraph letter(s) where each idea is mentioned.

a) the location of the Tenere desert ✓ _A_

b) a description of the landscape ☐ ....

c) a description of the plants which grow there ☐ ....

d) information about the history of the region ☐ ....

e) an example of an animal which lived there ☐ ....

f) details about the people who lived there in the past ☐ ....

g) a description of the homes of the people who lived there ☐ ....

h) information about the skills of the people who lived there ☐ ....

3a Read the sentence below which summarises an idea from the text. Which paragraph(s) is it from?

The .... of animal remains belonging to aquatic species shows that the Tenere desert once contained water

Paragraph ....

3b Choose the best word to complete the sentence in exercise 3a. Think about:

a) Whether the noun form (countable, uncountable or plural) goes with the main verb in the sentence (shows).

b) Whether the meaning matches the ideas in the text.

> **A** tests   **B** discovery   **C** position

> **Exam tip**
>
> When you have to choose words from a box to complete a summary, the words will usually all be of the same type: all nouns, all adjectives or all verbs. Look carefully for other grammatical clues such as whether nouns and verbs agree; you will need a plural noun with a plural verb form, for example.

4 Complete the gaps with the words in the box. You do not need all the words. First find the idea in the text. Then choose a word from the box to complete the gap. Think about both meaning and grammar.

> appearance   disappearance   evidence   ~~formation~~   inhabitants   objects   rise   society

1 The *formation* of a lake in the Tenere desert region 12,000 years ago was what enabled plants and animals to live there.

2 The first human .... of the Tenere desert were a people called the Kiffians.

3 Many of the .... which were found suggest that Kiffians got food by hunting and fishing.

4 It is thought that the Kiffians were forced to move away from the area for a short time due to a .... in the level of the lake.

5 The .... of the Kiffians from the area dates to around 8,000 years ago, when it returned to dry desert conditions.

> **Exam tip**
>
> There will be more words in the box than you need. Some will have a similar meaning. For each gap, choose the words that match the meaning in the text, then eliminate those which don't fit grammatically.

✏️ EXAM TASK: Reading (summary completion)

5 **Complete the summary. Write ONE word from the box in each gap.**

~~characteristics~~ differences evidence feature production signs similarity survival

The two ancient people who lived in the Tenere desert shared some **1** _characteristics_ . Both relied largely on catching wild animals for their **2** .... There is also **3** .... that both groups created sophisticated pottery at a time before its **4** .... was widespread in Europe and Asia. The **5** .... between the two groups include their physical appearance – Tenerians were taller and more strongly built – and also their use of agriculture; it seems that only the Tenerians kept domestic cattle.

PEOPLE OF THE TENERE DESERT

A The Ancient Egyptians, who lived on the edge of the Sahara desert, have been studied by many archaeologists. In the rest of Africa, however, large areas of desert have been studied very little, because it is difficult for humans to live in such a hot, dry climate. One of these places is the Tenere Desert, which stretches from North Eastern Niger to Western Chad. There are hardly any plants there and the temperature can reach over 40 degrees. The area is known by the Tuareg people who live in the region as the 'desert inside a desert'.

B But the Tenere was not always like this. In 2000, a team of researchers travelled to the area to study the remains of various extinct animal species which had once lived there. During their research, they left the flat desert to explore an area of sand dunes. This contained hundreds of remains, but not of creatures normally found in a desert. Rather, they were of aquatic creatures, such as an ancient crocodile known as *sarcosuchus*. Even more surprisingly, many of the remains in this landscape were human.

C The conditions of the Tenere desert today are very like those in the Pleistocene period, around 16,000 years ago. However, between then and now there seem to have been two periods when the area changed from being a barren desert to one covered with plants. The first period occurred about 12,000 years ago and was caused by a small change in the Earth's movement around the Sun. This brought rainfall to new areas. In this region a lake was formed, and the area soon became inhabited* by people. The first population who lived here are known as the Kiffians. Small pieces of tools and weapons have shown that they survived by hunting animals and fishing. They seem to have left the site temporarily on at least one occasion when the lake rose and caused floods. But the site was abandoned completely about 8,000 years ago, when the dry conditions returned and the area became desert again.

D Around one thousand years later, the area experienced another change in climate. Once again, it turned into grassland surrounding a lake, although probably one less deep than before. Consequently, it became inhabited by humans for a second time. This second group were the Tenerians. Whereas the Kiffians were very tall, sometimes nearly 2 metres, and very strong and muscular, the Tenerians were shorter, and much less robust. Analysis of bones has shown that the Kiffians were related to other groups across North Africa. The Tenerians, however, were biologically different and appear to have been closer to Mediterranean people. Like the Kiffians, they probably survived mainly through hunting and fishing, but the bones of cattle have also been found dating from this period. It would therefore seem that they kept domestic animals.

E Both groups of people apparently made pottery. This is remarkable for a population as ancient as the Kiffians and may mean that they were among the first people in Europe and Asia to do so. Analysis of pieces from pots found at the site has indicated two different styles. Pots with a zigzag design are Kiffian while the Tenerians produced pottery with a pattern of dots. The Tenerians clearly also made items of jewellery, as a bracelet made of hippo teeth has been found. More expeditions are likely to be organised to the area to look for further clues about the lifestyle of the two populations and, in particular, how they coped when the climate was starting to change.

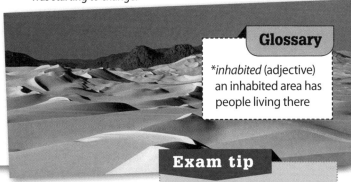

Glossary

*inhabited (adjective) an inhabited area has people living there

Exam tip

If you find an unknown word in a text, you can often work out the meaning if it is part of a contrast. For example: *The remains were not of creatures normally found in a desert. **Rather**, they were of <u>aquatic</u> creatures such as an ancient crocodile.*

6 **Scan the passage for the following words. Each one is part of the contrast. Use the contrast to choose the correct meaning, A or B.**

1 dunes (paragraph B) _A_
   A land which is hilly **B** land which is flat

2 barren (paragraph C) ....
   A with plants **B** without plants

3 temporarily (paragraph C) ....
   A for a short period of time **B** permanently

4 robust (paragraph D) ....
   A strong **B** not strong

5 zigzag (paragraph E) ....
   A a type of circle
   B a type of line

Global gardening

1a **Think of a garden or park you have visited. Make notes on the following:**

- the best season to visit it
- what you can see and do there
- the last time you visited it
- one change you would make to improve it

1b **Work in pairs to talk about your answer to exercise 1a. Use your notes to help you.**

2 **Read the summary and write the correct word type for each gap: noun, comparative adjective, verb or adverb.**

1 _comparative adjective_ **2** .... **3** .... **4** ....

If the climate becomes warmer, grass will probably experience a **1** _longer_ growing season than before. This is because winter rainfall is likely to **2** .... At the same time, more **3** .... will be needed due to changes in the patterns of this rainfall and the fact that it will tend to evaporate more **4** ....

> ### Exam tip
>
> You can sometimes tell the word type (noun, adjective, etc.) by looking at its suffix, e.g. the -tion ending means that it is a noun. This means you can often identify a possible answer for a gap even if you are not sure of the word's exact meaning.

3 **Decide which of the words in the box could go in each gap in exercise 2. There are TWO possible words for each gap.**

> **A** slowly **B** shorter **C** decrease **D** ~~longer~~
> **E** fertiliser **F** quickly **G** increase **H** irrigation

> ### Exam tip
>
> In a multiple-choice sentence completion exercise, the words in the box will not always be in the passage (although some of them may be). You will need to look for the same meaning in the passage expressed in different words.

4 **Scan the main passage for a paragraph about the idea in exercise Then read it carefully and complete exercise 2 with the correct words from exercise 3.**

✏ EXAM TASK: Reading (summary completion)

5 **Complete the sentences in the summary. Read the paragraph and the words in the box. Then decide on the possible answers before you read the passage.**

Climate change is likely to affect a number of popular garden plants and trees. Reduced amounts of **1** _rainfall_ will make it more difficult to grow some common garden plants, and some trees, such as the beech, may be affected by more frequent instances of **2** .... Conifer trees require relatively **3** .... temperatures in summer and so they may be particularly stressed. The changes may also result in poorer harvests of some **4** .... crops.

> **A** high **B** drought **C** wind **D** low **E** sunlight
> **F** fruit **G** flooding **H** ~~rainfall~~ **I** vegetable **J** Mediterranean

6 **Scan the passage for the words in the box. Then match them with the correct statements (1–4). There is one item you will not use.**

> **A** lupins **B** pine trees **C** lilies **D** cherry trees **E** oak trees

1 They will suffer more from water-borne diseases. ....

2 They will suffer from increased numbers of pests. ....

3 They will be affected by drier summers. _A_

4 They will be affected by hotter summers. ....

7a You can sometimes work out the meaning of a word by looking at its context. Read the following example:

> Some plants require permanent moisture in the soil and will not react well to long periods of dry weather

If the plants will not react well to *dry weather*, what do they require? What is, therefore, the meaning of *moisture*?

7b Scan the text for the following words. Then use the context to write a definition or translation of them.

a) drought (paragraph C) ....

b) thrive (paragraph C) ....

c) pest (paragraph E) ....

d) vulnerable (paragraph F) ....

Gardening and climate change

Glossary

horticulturist: an expert in the science of growing flowers, fruit or vegetables

lupins

blackberries

beech leaves

yew tree

A Any gardener will tell you that gardens sometimes suffer damage from unusual weather conditions. But in the last 20 or 30 years, the threat of climate change has meant that our gardens are facing a new threat. There may need to be permanent changes in the types of plants that can be grown, and gardeners may need to change their practices.

B One of the most familiar features of gardens in much of Europe are the green areas of closely cut grass. However, even a small rise in temperatures is likely to affect their growing patterns. Climate change means that it is likely that grass growth will take place during an increased number of months. Climate scientists also predict higher rainfall during the winter, which will lead to further growth. At the same time, the rain is likely to be heavier and concentrated in shorter periods, with longer dry periods between them. As a result, this will not mean less irrigation; rather, large areas of grass will need increased watering as the rate of evaporation will be higher.

C When it comes to garden plants and trees, a warmer climate may mean some of the plants traditionally associated with European gardens may become rare. A number of them, such as lupins, require permanent moisture in the soil and will not react well to long periods of dry weather and decreased rainfall. These periods of drought will also be damaging for some of our native trees, such as beech. This will mean that many of our parks, gardens and larger areas of woodland will look different in future. Many coniferous trees such as pines will not do well in the hotter temperatures that we face today, as they need cool summers to thrive.

D Some of the items typically grown in the domestic fruit and vegetable garden may also need to be replaced. Cherry trees and a number of berries, such as blackberries and raspberries, require cold weather over the winter months to stimulate their growth in the Spring. If winters become warmer, then this process will not take place, resulting in reduced crops. On the other hand, there may be new opportunities for Northern European gardeners to change to other types of fruit more associated with a Mediterranean climate, like figs. Both gardeners and farmers will need to adapt to these changes.

E Another negative consequence of climate change will be that some destructive insects and diseases will become more common. A particular concern is the scarlet beetle, which feeds on the leaves of plants in the lily family and is often a problem for horticulturists*. This pest has spread rapidly during the recent hot summers and will probably become even more numerous in future. Increased winter rainfall will also allow diseases that are carried in floodwater to spread more widely and attack greater numbers of trees such as oak and yew.

F It is likely that many gardeners will simply avoid these problems by choosing different types of plants. It is gardens which have a historical importance that are the real concern. Climate change means that it will be difficult to maintain them as they are now, and so a number of studies have provided risk assessments of the gardens in the most vulnerable sites. Some historical gardens may be saved, but for others the costs may be too great. In this case, they may have to be allowed to gradually change into a different environment more suited to the climate of the 21st century.

The *Rongorongo* script

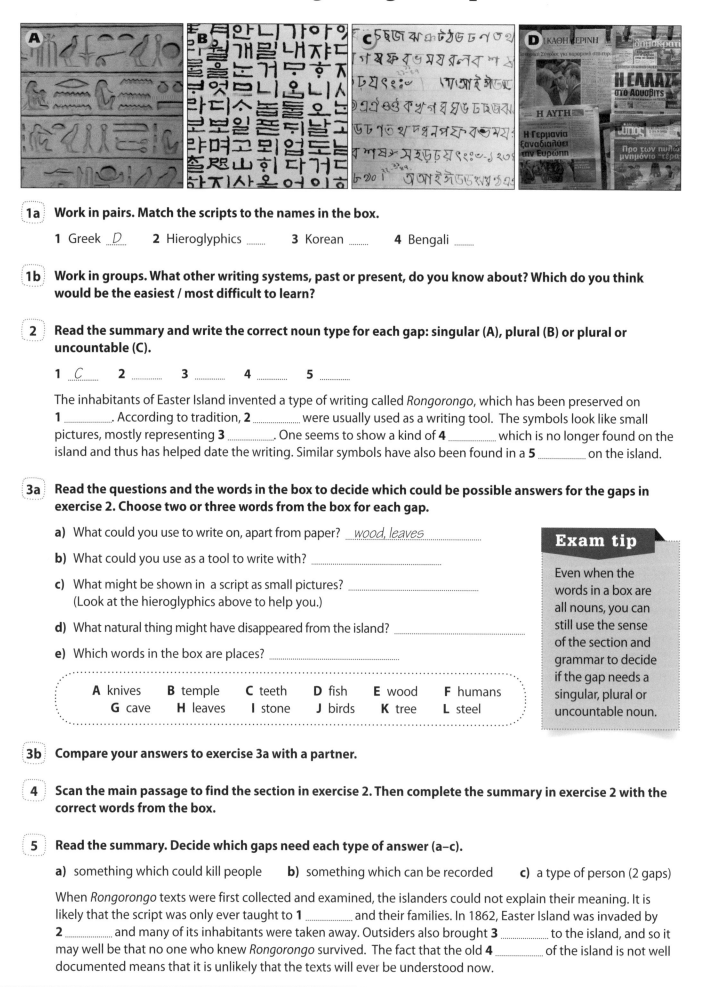

1a Work in pairs. Match the scripts to the names in the box.

1 Greek *D*   **2** Hieroglyphics ....   **3** Korean ....   **4** Bengali ....

1b Work in groups. What other writing systems, past or present, do you know about? Which do you think would be the easiest / most difficult to learn?

2 Read the summary and write the correct noun type for each gap: singular (A), plural (B) or plural or uncountable (C).

1 *C*   **2** ....   **3** ....   **4** ....   **5** ....

The inhabitants of Easter Island invented a type of writing called *Rongorongo*, which has been preserved on **1** .... According to tradition, **2** .... were usually used as a writing tool. The symbols look like small pictures, mostly representing **3** .... One seems to show a kind of **4** .... which is no longer found on the island and thus has helped date the writing. Similar symbols have also been found in a **5** .... on the island.

3a Read the questions and the words in the box to decide which could be possible answers for the gaps in exercise 2. Choose two or three words from the box for each gap.

a) What could you use to write on, apart from paper? *wood, leaves*

b) What could you use as a tool to write with? ....

c) What might be shown in a script as small pictures? ....
(Look at the hieroglyphics above to help you.)

d) What natural thing might have disappeared from the island? ....

e) Which words in the box are places? ....

> **Exam tip**
>
> Even when the words in a box are all nouns, you can still use the sense of the section and grammar to decide if the gap needs a singular, plural or uncountable noun.

A knives	**B** temple	**C** teeth	**D** fish	**E** wood	**F** humans
G cave	**H** leaves	**I** stone	**J** birds	**K** tree	**L** steel

3b Compare your answers to exercise 3a with a partner.

4 Scan the main passage to find the section in exercise 2. Then complete the summary in exercise 2 with the correct words from the box.

5 Read the summary. Decide which gaps need each type of answer (a–c).

a) something which could kill people   **b)** something which can be recorded   **c)** a type of person (2 gaps)

When *Rongorongo* texts were first collected and examined, the islanders could not explain their meaning. It is likely that the script was only ever taught to **1** .... and their families. In 1862, Easter Island was invaded by **2** .... and many of its inhabitants were taken away. Outsiders also brought **3** .... to the island, and so it may well be that no one who knew *Rongorongo* survived. The fact that the old **4** .... of the island is not well documented means that it is unlikely that the texts will ever be understood now.

PHOTOCOPIABLE

✎ EXAM TASK: Reading (summary completion)

6 Read the main passage and complete the summary in exercise 5 with the correct words from the box.

> **A** Europeans **B** place name **C** calendar **D** history
> **E** rulers **F** society **G** language **H** slave dealers
> **I** pictures **J** diseases **K** weapons **L** priests

The *Rongorongo* script of Easter Island

A Easter Island in the South Eastern Pacific Ocean is most famous today for the large statues which were created by its original inhabitants. But, in addition to these, it seems that this island nation also created a form of written script, similar to Egyptian hieroglyphics. Some people have argued that this script may have been brought to the island from South America, but this seems improbable, as Easter Island is such a remote place. It seems more likely that it was invented by the islanders. This was an extraordinary development as no other society in the South Pacific seems to have had any form of writing.

B The script is called *Rongorongo*, from the verb 'recite' in the island's language. All of the examples which survive today are written on wooden tablets, although there is a tradition that banana leaves were also used to write on. Tradition also states that the written characters were typically made by using shark teeth as cutting tools. The writing on one or two *Rongorongo* tablets looks as if it was made with a steel knife. These may therefore not be authentic.

C *Rongorongo* is written from the bottom to the top of each tablet. The script consists of symbols, the majority of which seem to show human figures, although there are a number of birds, animals and fish, and also some abstract shapes. One symbol seems to show a type of palm tree which disappeared from the island as deforestation took place. If so, this means that the script must have existed before this. Symbols which look like *Rongorongo* have also been found on the walls of a cave on the island.

D Tablets covered with the script were first noticed by outsiders in the 1860s. In that same decade Hippolyte Roussel, a priest living on the island, attempted to collect them and examine them. However, he only found a small number and was

surprised to discover that the local people seemed to have little interest in them. They were using the wooden tablets to make fires or for other purposes, like building boats. Moreover, none of them could agree what the symbols meant. It seems that literacy, as in many early societies, was not widespread, and writing was only taught to the ruling classes and their families. Clearly something had happened to prevent them from passing this knowledge to future generations.

E The event in question was almost certainly the attacks made on the island by Peruvian slave dealers, especially one in 1862 in which over a thousand islanders were captured or killed. These probably included most or all of the people who could write *Rongorongo*. A further factor may have been the introduction of deadly diseases such as smallpox by European explorers, which reduced the island's population even more.

F *Rongorongo* therefore remains unread, except for part of one tablet which has been shown to refer to a calendar. The fact that much of the old language of the island has been lost means that it will probably never be read now. Experts disagree about whether it was a true writing system with symbols that represented words. It may have been more like a pictorial record to help the memory of chiefs and storytellers and allow them to pass on facts about the island's history. Whichever it was, the information it contains is now almost certainly lost for ever.

7 **Find words in the passage with the following meanings.**

a) genuine, not false or copied (paragraph B) *authentic*

b) consisting of shapes and patterns, not real objects (paragraph C) ....

c) the ability to read and write (paragraph D) ....

d) existing among many people (paragraph D) ....

e) caught and kept as prisoners (paragraph E) ....

f) something that causes a situation (paragraph E) ....

Material origins

1a Work in pairs. Which of the materials in the box are natural fibres for cloth and which are man-made?

> acrylic   cotton   nylon   polyester   silk   wool

1b Which of the materials in exercise 1 come from the following sources?

2 Match the words with the correct definition (A–E). What are the past forms of the verbs in the exercise?

1 a mill   A to make cloth by crossing threads under and over each other

2 textiles   B to colour something such as cloth, using a special substance

3 to weave   C a building that produces materials such as cotton, cloth or steel

4 to spin   D any types of cloth that are made in large quantities

5 to dye   E to twist fibres of materials like cotton or silk into thin strings so that cloth can be made

3 Work in pairs. Ask and answer the questions.

a) What kind of textiles or clothes are traditionally produced in your country?

b) How important is textile making for the country's economy?

c) Are there any famous companies or brands which produce textiles or clothing in your country?

d) Was this different in the past? Why?

4a Read the summary and write the correct word type for each gap: singular noun, plural noun, uncountable noun / -*ing* form or adjective.

1 *adjective*   2 ....   3 ....   4 ....   5 ....

Early British attempts to cultivate mulberry trees for rearing silkworms were not successful because of the **1** *damp* climate. There was a small silk industry in London run by French immigrants, many of whom were skilled **2** .... However, the silk they used was obtained from abroad.

In the 18th century, Thomas Cotchett attempted to establish a **3** .... for producing silk, but this failed as he did not have the right equipment and the necessary **4** .... for silk manufacture were not generally known in Britain. John Lombe, one of his employees, therefore decided to find out what methods were used in Italian silk mills. As these were a trade secret, **5** .... was the only way to do this.

4b Compare your answers with a partner. How did you know the type of word that was needed?

5 Scan the main passage to find the section summarised in exercise 4a. Complete the summary. Write ONE WORD ONLY in each gap.

> ### Exam tip
>
> A sentence completion summary will not usually summarise the whole of a passage. Choose a good 'scanning' word, like a name or date, at the beginning of the summary so that you can look for it in the text and identify where the information in the sentence completion paragraph begins. You may be able to do the same with a word towards the end of the sentence completion summary.

✎ EXAM TASK: Reading (summary completion)

6 **Complete the summary. Decide what kind of word can go in each gap before you begin. Write ONE or TWO words in each gap.**

Lombe's silk mill contained machinery similar to that used in Italy and was powered by a number of **1** ....
It must also have contained a **2** .... as silk twisting can only be carried out in a warm environment.
Soon after the mill was opened, John Lombe died, possibly as a result of **3** .... The business was taken over by his brother, Thomas, and became very successful.

The original mill was destroyed in 1910. It has been rebuilt, but it now serves as a **4** ....

The beginnings of the British silk industry

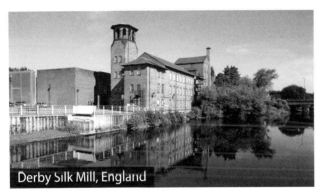
Derby Silk Mill, England

For many centuries the manufacture of silk in Europe was centred in France and Italy. Silk remained a rare material in Britain, although there were a few early attempts to start a native silk industry. In the 1600s, King James I had an area of mulberry trees planted, with a view to using them to rear silkworms (the worms only eat mulberry leaves), and asked a number of landowners to do the same. However, the damp weather meant that the leaves did not grow quickly enough and he abandoned the attempt. There was also a small centre for silk production based in London, but it was carried out by immigrants from France. Many of them were good weavers and had set up their own businesses producing silk and cotton cloth. They worked with silk which had been produced and spun in France and was only available at very high prices.

It was not until the 18th century that this situation really changed. At that time, a lawyer, Thomas Cotchett, became interested in the possibility of manufacturing silk and he set up a mill near the town of Derby. The project was unsuccessful because Cotchett did not possess the right equipment, and the techniques for producing silk were not common knowledge in Britain. The attempt might have ended there if it had not been for the actions of John Lombe, one of his employees.

Lombe believed that he could set up a silk industry in Britain if he could acquire knowledge of the techniques used in Italian silk manufacturing. The problem was that these techniques were a closely guarded secret. Therefore, he set out for Italy hoping to somehow gain access to one of the silk mills. His story is of interest as it is one of the first cases in which a new industry was created as a result of spying.

After a few months, Lombe was given a job in one of the silk mills, probably because he offered money to one of the workers there. This allowed him to watch the workings of the mill and make secret drawings of the machinery. These were returned to Britain using secret agents based in the port of Livorno. Eventually, rumours began to go around that someone was spying on the silk mill and Lombe quickly left the country.

His plan had succeeded, however, as he now had knowledge of the methods of Italian silk production. He built a new mill on the same site as Cotchett's earlier attempt. New machinery was created on the Italian model, which used energy from a series of waterwheels. The building also apparently had some form of heating system, as the silk-making process needs high temperatures to work.

Soon after the opening of the mill, John Lombe suddenly died. According to a popular story, this was because he was given poison by an Italian woman. She had been sent to England to take revenge on him for stealing the secrets of the silk-making trade. The factory continued to be run successfully by his brother, Thomas Lombe, and English silk began to build up a reputation for excellence, both at home and abroad.

The mill continued to run until 1910, when it was damaged by fire. Today nothing of Lombe's original building remains. However, it has been rebuilt and now it is used to house a museum of industry.

7 **Complete the definitions with a different verb from the passage which means the same thing. In some cases you will need verb + preposition.**

a) give up the attempt = _abandon_ the attempt

b) establish a business = ... a business

c) gain knowledge = ... knowledge

d) establish a reputation = ... a reputation

e) have an important role = ... an important role

Letting off steam

1 Work in pairs. Complete the table with the words in the box. Use a dictionary if necessary.

	feature	location
Grand Canyon		
Angel Falls		
Mount Everest	*mountain*	
Mount Vesuvius		
Quelccaya Ice Cap		*Peru*
Old Faithful		

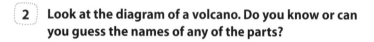

geyser   glacier   Italy   ~~mountain~~   Nepal   ~~Peru~~
USA (x2)   valley   Venezuela   volcano   waterfall

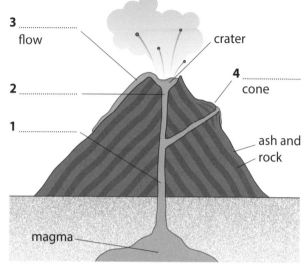

3 .... flow
crater

4 ....
cone

2 ....

1 ....

ash and rock

magma

2 Look at the diagram of a volcano. Do you know or can you guess the names of any of the parts?

✎ EXAM TASK: Reading (diagram label completion)

3 Read the description of a volcano and label the diagram in exercise 2. Use ONE word for each gap.

Exam tip

Remember a gap before a noun in a sentence is often an adjective but it can be another noun (to create a compound noun).

A volcano is formed when liquid rock underground (magma) finds its way to the earth's surface in a volcanic eruption. The part of the volcano that we see is formed of layers of ash and rock from previous eruptions.

Before an eruption occurs, pressure from underground causes magma to rise from its chamber deep under the earth. It is forced up through the conduit in the middle of the volcano until it reaches the area just below the opening at the top. This area is known as the throat of the volcano. From here, ash, gas and magma shoot up into the disc-shaped crater just above. The magma also frequently flows down the side of the volcano, and in this case it is referred to as lava. Occasionally, it may also find its way to a smaller opening at the side of the volcano and may even form a small cone there, which is said to be parasitic on the main cone.

4a Look at the title of the main passage and the picture. Which of the following words do you think will be in the passage?

geothermal   ice   jungle   petrol   steam   tourists   water

4b Work in pairs to compare your ideas. Then scan the passage to check.

✎ EXAM TASK: Reading (diagram label completion)

5 Read the passage and find the paragraph which describes how a geyser works. Then label the diagram. Use ONE or TWO words for each gap.

Exam tip

In a diagram-labelling question, the words to complete the gaps may not appear in the same order in the passage as they appear in the diagram.

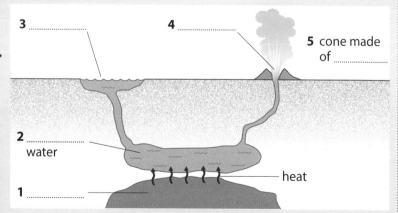

3 ....

4 ....

5 cone made of ....

2 ....
water

1 ....

heat

6 Scan the passage for the geysers in the box. Then match them with the correct statements (1–5). There is one item you will not use.

> **A** The Steamboat Geyser   **B** Old Faithful   **C** The Lady Knox Geyser
> **D** The Waimangui Geyser   **E** The Fly Geyser   **F** The Minute Geyser

1 Its force has been weakened by the activity of visitors. _F_

2 It stopped erupting after a natural event. ....

3 It is made to erupt regularly for tourists. ....

4 it was created by human activity. ....

5 It currently shoots water higher than any other geyser. ....

Letting off steam:
A survey of the world's geysers

A Geysers are natural events in which boiling water from under the ground is forced to the Earth's surface, and shoots up into the air. They are fairly uncommon as their formation depends on particular conditions underground. There are two basic types: cone geysers and fountain geysers.

B In cone geysers, the spot where the water comes out is fairly small and has a cone shaped formation around it. Their eruptions tend to be powerful, with a continual jet of water. The tallest active geyser in the world, the Steamboat in Yellowstone Park, USA, is an example of this type. Another is Old Faithful, probably the most famous geyser in the park. Fountain geysers have a larger vent at the surface that fills with water before an eruption. They are usually less high and the water tends to shoot out irregularly.

C In both types of geyser, the eruption is caused by the same process. Water is heated by magma underground. If it can flow freely to the surface, it forms a pool or lake of hot water, known as a hot spring. If, however, there are bends or tight places along the path to the surface, the water remains underground. With no space to turn to steam, it becomes superheated under pressure. Eventually, the water underneath makes its way upwards with great force, coming out through a vent on the Earth's surface. The cones of cone geysers are formed because the water frequently makes its way through volcanic rocks which are rich in silica (an element which is often found in magma). This is dissolved so that it becomes part of the hot water but then cools and becomes solid around the vent.

D Many geysers are popular tourist attractions, although the fact that they are unpredictable can be a problem. This is why Old Faithful, whose eruptions take place so regularly, is so popular. Most, however, are unreliable and can be inactive for long periods. It is possible to cause a few of them to erupt by adding soap, which breaks the surface tension on the water. The Lady Knox Geyser in New Zealand, for example, is made to eject water in this way every morning for the benefit of visitors.

E As geysers need very specific conditions, they can easily be destroyed by changes underground or on the Earth. Volcanic activity, earthquakes and abnormal patterns of rainfall can all have an effect. The Waimangu Geyser, for example, was once the highest in the world, but a landslide changed the position of the water underground and it is now no longer active. Humans have also played their part in destroying the world's geysers, either through tourism or their search for new forms of energy. Sometimes this has actually caused a new geyser to form, like the Fly Geyser in Nevada. This was created as a result of drilling into the earth as part of a project to create a geothermal power plant. More often, however, projects like this cause damage to geysers as they steal their water and lower the pressure underground. Tourism has also had undesirable effects. The Minute Geyser in Yellowstone Park was located next to a coach stop and the waiting tourists liked to throw coins into it. This eventually blocked the geyser so that its eruptions, which were once 12 to 15 metres high, are now only about a metre in height.

7a **Read the passage again. Find the opposites of the adjectives in the passage.**

   a) common _uncommon_   **c)** predictable ....   **e)** active ....

   b) regular ....   **d)** reliable ....   **f)** normal ....

7b **Work in pairs. Think of more adjectives with the prefixes _un-_, _in-_, and _ir-_.**

Designed for disaster

1   Work in groups. Discuss the different types of buildings. Use the questions below.

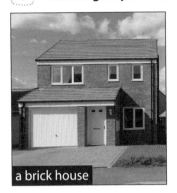
a brick house

a concrete block of flats

a glass skyscraper

a wooden house

     a) Which types of building are most common where you live?

     b) Which type of building would you prefer to live in?

     c) What are the advantages and disadvantages of each type of building?

2   Read the main passage quickly and note the topic(s) of each section. Use the ideas in the box or your own words.

> building design   building materials   a design competition   how earthquakes affect buildings
> how earthquakes happen   researching and testing   a severe earthquake   young designers

3   Match the highlighted parts of these words from the passage to the definitions.

1   quake-**proof**

2   home**less**

3   **un**safe, **un**damaged, **un**reinforced

4   afford**able**

5   **super**computer

A not

B bigger / better than usual

C protecting against

D that can be done

E without

> **Exam tip**
>
> Prefixes at the start of words (*un-*) and suffixes at the end of words (*-proof*, *-less*) can help you to work out the meaning of unfamiliar words in a text.

4a   Read section B of the passage again. Underline the sentences which describe the steps in the table below. Ignore the gaps at this stage.

	Action	Result
Step 1	**1** .... hit each other	an earthquake
Step 2	**2** .... spread out from the epicentre	the surface of the earth moves up and down and side **4** ....
Step 3	structures, such as buildings, sway **3** .... than usual	the buildings are put under great **5** .... and may collapse

4b   Read the instruction below, then choose the best phrase (a–c) to complete gap 1 in the table in exercise 4a.

> Complete the table. Choose NO MORE THAN TWO WORDS from the passage for each answer.

> **Exam tip**
>
> The information needed to complete a table will usually come from only one part of the passage. Use key words in the table to help you find the relevant section of the passage.

> **a** giant pieces of rock   **b** tectonic plates   **c** geological plates

4c   Work in pairs. Choose words from the passage to complete the other gaps in the table in exercise 4a.

5a   Look at the table. What is the main topic? Identify which section of the passage describes this topic.

Quake-proof home

A   On January 12, 2010, a massive earthquake hit the Caribbean island nation of Haiti near its capital, Port-au-Prince. The 7.0-magnitude earthquake destroyed more than 100,000 buildings and caused an estimated $8 billion worth of damage. More than 316,000 people were killed. It was one of the deadliest earthquakes in recorded history, and 1.5 million people were left homeless.

News of the disaster hit home for a student in Ohio, USA. Just months earlier, Ashton Cofer had met a group of students who were visiting the USA from Haiti. He soon learned that his Haitian friends were safe, but he still wanted to help victims of future earthquakes. Ashton teamed up with school friends Julie Bray and Luke Clay to invent a quake-proof house. They wanted to design a structure that wouldn't collapse in an earthquake, thereby reducing fatalities and preventing people from becoming homeless.

B   The Earth's crust is like a jigsaw puzzle made of tectonic plates. These giant pieces of rock are always moving slowly, and an earthquake occurs as plates rub together. An earthquake's epicentre is the area on Earth's surface directly above where the plates collide. Seismic waves move outwards from the epicentre like ripples on water. The seismic waves move up and down and side to side in a motion that causes objects on Earth's surface to sway and shift.

'You might not be able to see it, but buildings are always moving back and forth due to natural forces like wind,' says Patrick McCafferty, a structural engineer. During earthquakes, structures on land sway much faster than under normal conditions, and this puts them under great strain.

C   To overcome these forces, a building must be constructed with strong, flexible* materials that have a high tensile strength. That's the amount of force material can withstand being stretched or pulled without breaking. Solid steel girders and reinforced concrete – a network of thin steel rods inside concrete – are both strong and flexible building materials. But they're also expensive. Haiti is the poorest country in the western hemisphere, and many of its structures are designed with cheap, unsafe materials. 'We learnt that most of the destruction in Haiti occurred because many of the buildings are made of unreinforced concrete,' says Julie. 'Concrete has a very low tensile strength.' It buckles* easily.

Ashton, Julie, and Luke searched for a material that could resist an earthquake's force, but still be affordable. The students settled on a species of strong, flexible bamboo which grows in the Caribbean. This type of bamboo grows fast – to a height of about 20 metres in only 4 to 6 months – and sells for one tenth the cost of concrete.

D   Next they researched buildings and other products designed to withstand strong vibrations*. They found a surprisingly strong item: the Pringles potato chip. 'A Pringles potato chip is in the shape of a hyperbolic paraboloid,' says Luke. "They were designed by supercomputers to reduce breakage during transport.'

The team decided to use this curved shape to make a prototype model home from bamboo. They joined bent pieces of bamboo together, using rubber bands at the joints. They tested the prototype in a lab against two concrete models on a shake table – a device that copies seismic waves. 'Both concrete houses failed catastrophically,' says Julie, 'but our house had no failures.'

E   The students entered their design, which they named the Quake Safe House, in a national competition which challenges high school students to propose a solution to a real-world problem. The team won the competition for their age group. The designs are now online so other inventors can improve on them. Their hope is that their project will help save the lives of people in future earthquakes.

Glossary

* *flexible* (adjective) able to bend easily without breaking
* *buckle* (verb) to twist and break
* *vibration* (noun) a shaking movement

✎ EXAM TASK: Reading (table completion)

5b   **Complete the table. Choose ONE WORD ONLY from the passage for each answer.**

Building Material	Cost	Characteristics
reinforced concrete	1	high tensile strength: strong and flexible
2 .... concrete	relatively cheap	3 .... tensile strength: buckles easily in an earthquake
4	more 5 .... for people in poor regions	strong and flexible

Exam tip

Read the instructions carefully. If it asks for 'no more than one word', you can use one word only in each gap. If it asks for 'no more than two words', you can use one word or two words in each gap.

PHOTOCOPIABLE ✄

Animal intelligence

1a Work in groups. Which of these animals do you think is intelligent? Discuss what you know about:

- how they communicate with each other
- how social they are
- their memory and ability to learn
- their ability to use tools
- whether they can recognise their own reflection in a mirror

1b Which of these abilities and characteristics do you think shows the most intelligence?

2 Skim the main passage and answer the questions.

a) Which paragraphs are mainly about the animal's anatomy (its body)? Which are about its intelligence and behaviour?

b) Overall, is the passage mainly about the octopus' anatomy or intelligence?

c) Which of the topics in exercise 1a are mentioned?

> **Exam tip**
>
> When wanting to get the general sense (or gist) of a passage, you can read it quickly to find out its main points without focusing on the details. This is called *skimming*.

3a Read the sentence beginnings and scan the passage for the underlined key words. Then note down the paragraph letter(s).

1 An octopus' <u>stomach</u> and other organs *B*

2 Two of its three <u>hearts</u> ....

3 Most of the animal's <u>brain</u> <u>cells</u> ....

4 The <u>suckers</u> on its <u>arms</u> ....

5 <u>Pigments</u> in an octopus' <u>skin</u> ....

> **Exam tip**
>
> Sometimes questions contain words which will be repeated in the passage. These are often proper nouns (names of people, places and organisations) or technical terms that would be difficult to change. (e.g. *heart, sucker*) These words are easy to scan for, so you may want to answer questions which contain them first.

3b Work in pairs. Read the information around the key words in the sentence beginnings in exercise 3a. How do you think each sentence will end?

3c Match the sentence beginnings in exercise 3a to the endings. You will not need all the endings. Explain to your partner why the unused endings were not correct.

A are in its arms rather than its 'head'.

B enable it to breathe.

C allow it to change colour.

D can taste and feel.

E are found in the sac behind its eyes.

F enable it to survive extreme temperatures.

G pump blood around its body.

> **Exam tip**
>
> Don't try to match the sentence parts in this type of question using grammar – they will probably all fit. Look at the sentence beginnings first and search for the same information in the passage. Then read the sentence endings and choose the meaning which matches the passage best.

✏ EXAM TASK: Reading (matching sentence endings)

4a **Read the sentence beginnings. Underline the key words and find the information in the passage.**

1 An octopus may use rocks ....

2 An octopus may take on the appearance of a rock ....

3 An octopus may disguise itself as a crab ....

4 An octopus may display a dark colour ....

5 An octopus shows a pale colour ....

4b **Complete each sentence in exercise 5a with the correct ending.**

A when it wants to catch food.

B if it wishes to scare another octopus.

C when it wants to avoid confrontation.

D when it wants to hide the entrance to its home.

E if it wishes to attract a mate.

F if it needs to hide from a predator.

The octopus decoded

A Octopuses are unlike any other creature on earth. Even their DNA contains a genetic code which, compared with other animals, seems to have been completely rearranged. This is no doubt why they show so many special characteristics.

B A description of an octopus' body makes it sound quite unreal. Humans might assume that the round blob* behind its eyes is its head. In fact, although the brain is located there, this is actually its body, containing the stomach, liver, kidney and its three hearts. Two of these hearts pump blood across the octopus' gills so it can breathe, and the third pumps it to the rest of the body. Perhaps most surprisingly, octopus blood is blue, and contains a substance, hemocyanin, which enables it to stay alive at hot and cold temperatures that would be deadly to most creatures.

C Octopuses are highly intelligent and have the biggest brains of any invertebrate* in comparison with their body weight. Their intelligence is also shown by the number of neurones (cells that process information) they have. A human brain has approximately 100 billion neurones, whereas that of an octopus has about 130 million. But that is not the whole story, because only a minority of an octopus' neurones are in its brain. More than three fifths are in its arms – almost as if each one had a mind of its own. The suckers that cover an octopus' arms are not just for gripping surfaces but can taste as well as touch. There is even some evidence that these arms may be able to see.

D Octopuses show many indications of intelligent behaviour. Laboratory experiments have shown they have excellent spatial memory and can remember the correct way through a complicated maze. Like the more intelligent birds and mammals, they also show signs of tool use. Jennifer Mather, a marine biologist, has recorded how one octopus found three correctly-sized rocks which it arranged in front of its den to hide the opening before going to sleep.

E Much of an octopus' intelligence, however, allows it to hide from predators by changing shape and colour to avoid being killed. Its skin is loaded with special cells known as chromatophores. These contain pigments which can be pushed to the surface, allowing an octopus to adopt three or four different colours. As well as changing its skin colour, an octopus can alter its texture by making it bumpy or spiky. In this way, they can make themselves look like seaweed or a rock when sharks or other fish that like to eat them are nearby. Some even use this ability to trap food, transforming their bodies to look like tasty crabs to attract prey.

F This colour-changing ability also seems to be used to send messages. David Sheel of Alaska Pacific University has documented octopuses changing colour in order to signal to each other. An octopus displaying a dark colour seemed to be showing aggression* to another octopus. If the second octopus showed a similar colour then the two were likely to fight, whereas if it turned pale this seemed to be a signal that it was ready to back off.

G One reason why octopus intelligence is so different from human intelligence is that octopuses have a short lifespan and are non-social. Baby octopuses do not have contact with, or learn from, their parents. The challenge for human researchers, then, is how to get inside the minds of these creatures, whose intelligence has developed for a life of solitude*.

> **Glossary**
>
> *blob* (noun) something soft that is roughly round in shape
> *invertebrate* (noun) an animal with no bones inside its body
> *aggression* (noun) behaviour that shows it wants to fight with or harm another animal
> *solitude* (noun) being or living alone

Dealing with failure

1a Think of a person you know who is successful in their career. Make notes on:

- what they do
- why they have been successful
- how they arrived at where they are today
- whether they have experienced failures as well as successes.

1b Talk to a partner about the person you chose in exercise 1a. Use your notes to help you.

2a Choose the correct word from the box to complete the questions.

> fails   failure   succeed   ~~success~~   successful

a) Is it realistic to expect everyone to achieve _success_ in business?

b) How do people deal with .... when something goes wrong?

c) What should businesses do when a plan .... ?

d) Do we need to learn from our mistakes in order to .... ?

e) What is the most .... strategy for dealing with problems at work?

2b Discuss your answers to the questions in exercise 2a in groups.

3a Skim the main passage and note down the key idea for each paragraph.

3b Scan and underline the names and other key words in the sentences below.

1 According to Evelyn Krens, businesspeople who have gained a high position tend to focus more on their successes. _B, C_

2 In the aviation industry it is important for staff to report errors, but they are not punished if their mistakes were accidental. ....

3 After the introduction of the Six Sigma at 3M, scientists tended to experiment less. ....

4 Eli Lilly realised that learning from mistakes is important, but you also have to encourage a positive attitude. ....

4a Read the passage in more detail. Write down in which paragraph the information in each sentence in exercise 3b can be found.

4b Work in pairs or groups. Compare the sentences in exercise 3b to the same information in the reading passage. Discuss which paraphrasing technique(s) are used in each case.

a Using synonyms; words with a similar meaning,
  e.g. *who have gained a high position = who have climbed up the career ladder*

b Using different word forms

c Expressing an idea from a different perspective

d Summarising several ideas in a word or short phrase

Exam tip

The sentences in the questions will often paraphrase the ideas in the reading passage. Look out for different types of paraphrasing. Do the ideas in the question and those in the passage have the same meaning?

✏ EXAM TASK: Reading (matching sentence endings)

5a **Read the sentence beginnings. Find the information in the passage. Use the key words to help you.**

1 According to Evelyn Krens, some companies don't worry about minor failures ....

2 Companies can identify opportunities for staff training ....

3 In the 'Just Culture', employees are not punished for an error ....

4 Businesses sometimes experience failures ....

5 Peter Sims believes that companies will not develop in the future ....

Exam tip

The information in the incorrect sentence endings may be in the passage, but it won't match the first part of the sentence. Think about the meaning of the complete sentence – does it accurately match an idea in the passage?

5b **Complete each sentence with the correct ending.**

A if they keep a record of everyday mistakes.

B if they don't greatly affect their profits.

C when they break the rules on purpose.

D if they admit to it.

E because they don't pay attention to safety standards.

F if they concentrate only on short-term success.

G because they are exploring new ways of doing things.

Failure management

A There are many books giving advice on how to achieve success in business, but far fewer on dealing with failure. As most of us want to succeed this emphasis is understandable but, of course, the path to success will almost certainly involve failures along the way. Learning from these is probably more important than focusing on success alone.

B Many companies accept this, yet their staff are still unwilling to talk about mistakes and failures. Sometimes, indeed, a company may not want to find out why something went wrong. 'If one part of a company is making small losses, but the rest of it is making enough money to cover them, then they may be relatively unconcerned,' says Evelyn Krens, Professor of Management.

C The attitude of many managers does not encourage examination of failures. As Krens points out, people who have climbed high up the career ladder often push previous failures to the back of their minds. Senior management need to be aware of this and talk honestly about their projects that did not work. This will encourage staff to talk about their errors and discuss them freely. If a log is kept so that the company can see where problems most commonly occur, this can form the basis of a programme for staff development. Changing the way in which failure is referred to can also help. Staff are more likely to respond to enquiries about failures if impersonal questions like 'How did this happen?' are asked, instead of ones which invite blame, like 'Who did this?'

D Yet there is a dilemma here. Staff need to feel they can talk about their failures, but if there are no consequences, they may become irresponsible or careless about following rules. The aviation industry has tried to solve this problem by implementing a system called 'Just Culture'. This makes it an employee's responsibility to report any errors that they make. If they do this, then no disciplinary action is taken. However, this does not apply to cases where staff have deliberately disobeyed rules. The idea is to allow staff to learn from errors while making it clear that following the rules is still compulsory.

E This points to the fact that 'failure' is a broad concept. Often failures can arise from complicated situations which are genuinely difficult to handle. Other failures can be seen as exploratory – that is, they come about because they are part of the creative process or attempts to take a company in new directions. Companies which simply carry on with their normal activities and are afraid to try out new 'alleys' are focusing on immediate gain and losing sight of the bigger picture of business development. 3M, the American conglomerate, provides another example. At one point, this company introduced Six Sigma, a technique designed to eliminate errors on production lines, and applied it to all its activities, including the research laboratories. As a result, scientists working there lost their willingness to be creative and test out new possibilities for products.

F In general, companies are probably becoming better at analysing their failures. The pharmaceutical company Eli Lilly even used to hold 'failure parties' to honour scientists who came up with a promising suggestion that had failed in trials. Although positive in intention, this was probably a step too far as. Now they avoid the word 'failure' but continue to reward those who experiment and add to the company's knowledge, either by confirming or disproving a theory.

Harmful to health

1 **Work in groups. Discuss the following questions.**

   a) What causes pollution? (e.g. traffic)

   b) What are the effects of pollution on people and animals? (e.g. breathing problems)

2 **Read paragraph A of the passage and answer the questions.**

   a) Where is Cerro de Pasco?

   b) What is causing pollution in the city?

   c) What is the effect on the people who live there?

Swallowed by a mine

Residents of a city in Peru live with the effects of a huge, toxic lead mine.

Harmful expansion

A High in the Andes Mountains in Peru, a massive *mine is slowly taking over the 400-year-old city of Cerro de Pasco. It has left a huge hole in the centre of the city. The giant hole covers an area equal to that of about 240 football fields. It continues to expand, eating away at the town around its edge and forcing people from their homes. The mine is also having a negative impact on residents' health – by poisoning the environment with dangerous chemicals.

B Mining operations in Cerro de Pasco date back to the 1600s, when Spanish colonists discovered silver there. Later, the area was mined for copper. Until the 1950s, miners used tunnels to dig out these metals. Then the largest company mining the area switched to an open-pit mine to remove *lead and zinc. The company dug a huge hole instead of underground tunnels, but it happened that these metals lay directly under the town.

C As the mine expanded, workers dumped waste rock around the edges of the hole. The piles, full of toxic lead and other harmful metals, have grown to the size of small hills. Many lie just metres from houses and schools. Lead-filled dust blows everywhere in the city, and water that runs off from the mine has polluted nearby lakes and rivers, turning them an orange colour and leaving residents without safe drinking water.

Toxic metals effects

D Cecilia Chamorro, now 36, grew up in Cerro de Pasco, in a house just six metres from a pile. She didn't know how dangerous it could be until her son, Daniel, had a blood test at age two. 'He had 20 micrograms of lead per decilitre in his blood,' says Chamorro. That's four times the acceptable level identified by the US Centers for Disease Control and Prevention, although no amount of lead is considered safe.

E Lead is a neurotoxin, which means it affects the nervous system. It poses the greatest risk to children. Even low levels of lead can cause learning problems and behavioural issues.

Daniel, who is now 12, and his sister Araseli, 8, both have learning disabilities. High levels of lead can cause serious health problems and even death.

Town in need of help

F In places where lead is found in dust or soil, children are even more at risk, because they play on the floor or ground. They take in dust or soil containing lead when they put objects or their hands into their mouths, says Bruce Lanphier, a researcher at Simon Fraser University in Canada, who studies the effects of lead on children.

G Lead levels in Cerro de Pasco's children have been measured since 1996. In 2012, the Peruvian Health Ministry found that about 2,000 children had lead levels higher than twice the acceptable level. That was more than half of those children tested. Several measures have been proposed to help the residents, including improved healthcare facilities and even moving the town away from the mine altogether.

H But the plans have never been implemented as no one could decide who should pay for them. An American company owned the mine for more than half of the past century, then the Peruvian government and, most recently, a Peruvian company. It is therefore difficult to say who should be held responsible for the lead poisoning.

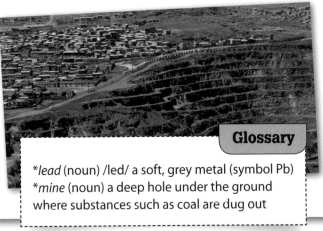

Glossary

lead (noun) /led/ a soft, grey metal (symbol Pb)
mine (noun) a deep hole under the ground where substances such as coal are dug out

3a Read the complete passage. Note down the paragraph letter each cause and effect is mentioned in.

Causes

1 _A_ The mine is expanding

2 ...... Water runs off from the mine

3 ...... Low levels of lead in the human body

4 ...... High levels of lead in the human body

5 ...... Children play on the ground

Effects

i Learning disabilities and behavioural problems ......

ii Serious health problems ......

iii There is no safe drinking water

iv People have to leave their homes ......

v Children put dusty hands in their mouths

vi Local rivers and lakes become polluted ......

3b Match the causes and effects in exercise 3a.

4 Work in pairs. Take turns to explain the cause and effect relationships in exercise 3a. Use the language in the box to link the ideas.

> to affect   as   at risk   because (of)   to cause   impact
> to pose a risk   responsible for   therefore

Water runs off from the mine and <u>causes</u> local lakes and rivers to turn orange.

> **Exam tip**
>
> Look for key words in a passage that show cause and effect relationships, e.g. *lead poisoning <u>caused by</u> the mine*. This will help you understand the overall opinion of the passage's writer.

5a Read the statements and scan the passage in one minute to find the key ideas. Write the correct paragraph letter.

1 The presence of toxic chemicals in Cerro de Pasco has badly affected residents' health. _A_   (T)/ F / NG

2 Only high levels of lead cause damage to the body's nervous system. ......   T / F / NG

3 Children are especially at risk from drinking polluted water. ......   T / F / NG

4 There is no money to help residents because current ownership of the mine is unclear. ......   T / F / NG

5b Read the information around the key ideas and think about the relationships expressed. Do they match the ideas in the passage? Decide whether the statement is true, false or not given.

> **Exam tip**
>
> If a statement *contradicts* information in the passage, the passage gives *different* information. In this case, the answer is 'false'. If you cannot find the information in the passage, the answer is 'not given'. Do not answer the question based on your own knowledge.

✎ EXAM TASK: Reading (identifying information)

6 Do the statements in exercise 5a agree with the information in the passage? Circle

TRUE   if the statement agrees with the information

FALSE   if the statement contradicts the information

NOT GIVEN if there is no information on this

Print your own ❶

A spool of plastic unwinds as the printer makes an object.

❷ Heated nozzles melt the plastic and squeeze it onto the platform to deposit a thin layer of plastic.

❸ The object is built layer by layer, until the printer has created a complete object.

1 Work with a partner. Which of these things do you regularly print out?

> coursework   online information   photos   timetables   travel tickets

2a Look at the diagram of a 3D printer. In pairs, discuss how you think a 3D printer is different from a traditional printer.

A traditional printer prints ink onto paper to create text or pictures. A 3D printer ...

2b Which of these things do you think can be made using a 3D printer?

> aeroplanes   boats   body parts   bones   bottles   buildings
> cars   clothes   computers   food   human hands
> mobile phone cases   TV remote controls

3a Scan the passage quickly. How many of the things in the box does it mention? Underline the words.

3b Work in pairs. Read the passage again and discuss the questions about each of the things in exercise 2b.

a) Can 3D printers print the whole object or just parts of it?

b) According to the passage, do people print the finished object or a model?

c) Is it possible to print this object now or might it be possible in the future?

Exam tip

It is helpful to scan a text for key words that appear in questions. Make sure you read the passage around the key word carefully to understand exactly what it says.

4a Complete the statements below about the passage, using the best word from the box.

> affordable ~~cheaper~~ complicated easy expensive inexpensively large miniature possible quickly smaller

a) Jim Smith's 3D-printed kayak was *cheaper* than one he could buy from a shop.

b) The early 3D printers were very .... and very ....

c) Now, 3D printers are much .... and much more ....

d) It has become .... for anyone to design and print something.

e) It is even .... to print some kinds of foods using a 3D printer.

f) Designers can use printed models to test their designs .... and ....

g) Architects can make .... models of buildings to see how they will look.

h) Doctors can practise .... operations using printed models of body parts.

5 Underline the adjectives and adverbs in the pairs of sentences. Do the pairs of sentences have the same or different meanings?

1 a The printers offer a way to make medical devices <u>cheaply</u>.

b Medical devices can be made <u>inexpensively</u> using 3D printers.

2 a One popular website has more than 100,000 free designs for users to download.

b There are more than 100,000 affordable designs that people can download from one site.

3 a Boeing estimates that more than 20,000 3D-printed parts currently fly on its planes.

b More than 20,000 parts made using 3D printers have actually been used in Boeing planes.

Exam tip

Adjectives and adverbs are often key to meaning. Compare the adjectives and adverbs used in the passage to those used in the questions. Do they have a similar meaning or a different meaning?

6a **Read the statements. Underline any adjectives and adverbs that are key to the meaning. Then look for similar information in the passage. Does the meaning match the statements?**

1 Jim Smith printed his own kayak much more cheaply than a shop-bought boat.   *True*

2 3D printers always use coloured plastic to create objects.   ....

3 The first 3D printers were difficult to use and only operated by experts.   ....

4 Now 3D printers are mostly used to create prototypes of products.   ....

5 3D-printed artificial hands are cheaper than what was available before.   ....

6 Scientists are already developing printers that will be able to print entire devices.   ....

✎ EXAM TASK: Reading (identifying information)

6b **Do the statements in exercise 6a agree with the information in the passage? Write:**

TRUE   if the statement agrees with the information

FALSE   if the statement contradicts the information

NOT GIVEN if there is no information on this

Just press print

3D printers have made their way into schools, hospitals and even into space. Where will they go next?

A Last Spring, mechanical engineer Jim Smith wanted to go kayaking near his home in South Carolina, USA. The only problem was he didn't have a kayak. Most people would have headed for a sports shop to buy or rent a boat, but Smith decided to print one. First, he designed a 5.5-metre-long kayak on his computer. Then he used a 3D printer in his garage to print 38 plastic pieces, which he assembled into a complete, functioning boat. It cost half the price of a similar store-bought kayak. Smith is a mechanical engineer at a company that sells 3D printers and 3D-printing products, but experts like Smith aren't the only ones making amazing creations with 3D printers. In the past five years, 3D printing has become much more common and more widely available.

B Conventional printers use ink to create text and images on paper, but 3D printers work differently. Many of them use colourful plastic as their printing material. The machine pushes strings of plastic through heated nozzles, melting the plastic and squeezing it onto a platform below. It adds layer after layer of plastic to build the object. But plastic isn't the only material used in 3D printers. Some use metal, ceramic, glass or wood. It's even possible to print 3D food! Printers can print powdered sugar mixtures in different colours and flavours, resulting in 3D-printed candy.

C Although 3D printers have been around since the mid-1980s, they've only recently become more affordable. In 2005, 3D printers were mostly industrial size and extremely expensive. Today it's possible to buy a small 3D printer for less than the cost of many computers.

D Another reason 3D printing has taken off is that it's become easy for anyone to design and print something, whether they're experts or not. One popular website has more than 100,000 free designs for users to download. If a user finds a design for a mobile phone case, for example, they can download the file, press print and watch their new phone case appear before their eyes.

E Increasingly, you don't have to look far to find 3D-printed objects around you. The aeroplane manufacturer Boeing estimates that more than 20,000 3D-printed parts currently fly on its planes. And while some objects come out of 3D printers ready to use, others are prototypes. These test models allow manufacturers to inexpensively and quickly see what their designs will look like in real life. Then they can make improvements before creating their finished products. Many of the products on store shelves – from shoes to shampoo bottles – likely started out as 3D-printed prototypes. Even architects print miniature versions of buildings they've designed to see how they look before starting construction.

F 3D printing is also directly improving people's lives. Doctors can use the printers to create metal implants to replace bones. They can even print replicas of patients' body parts to practise on before performing complicated operations. The printers also offer a way to make medical devices more quickly and cheaply. That's especially significant for children who need artificial limbs, because they have to replace them regularly as their bodies grow. Relatively inexpensive 3D-printed artificial hands or legs make these regular replacements possible for children from all backgrounds.

G Some scientists believe that eventually everyone will have a 3D printer in their home to make anything from food to furniture. 'Printing complete working devices, that's really the future,' says Hod Lipson, the director of the Creative Machines Lab in New York. 'If you need a new remote control, for example, you'll be able to just download and print.'

Picture this

1. **Work in groups. Discuss which of these activities would be inappropriate when visiting an art museum. Explain your reasons.**

   - taking photographs
   - eating or drinking
   - talking on your mobile phone
   - chatting to your friends about the pictures
   - touching the pictures

2. **Skim the passage below. What is being banned in some art museums and why?**

No Selfie Sticks

Many art museums are banning a popular device used to take self-portraits.

Picture this: you're admiring a painting at a museum, when suddenly a long, metal rod blocks your view. It's a selfie stick – a device that attaches to a smartphone so people can extend their reach to take more flattering pictures of themselves. A group is using the gadget to take a picture in front of the artwork. That's when a guard approaches and points to a sign which reads, 'No selfie sticks allowed.'

This scenario* is playing out in art museums around the world. The popularity of selfie sticks has led many museums – from the Metropolitan Museum of Art in New York to the National Gallery in London – to add selfie sticks to their lists of banned items. Museum officials worry that visitors wielding selfie sticks could accidentally damage priceless works of art. The sticks may even encourage bad manners, with many complaining that the devices are distracting to other museum goers. In

addition, people too focused on using the sticks to achieve the best photos might miss out on the real purpose of visiting a museum – enjoying the artworks on display.

Not everyone, however, is happy with the museums' new anti-selfie-stick rules. Some say that selfie sticks are no different from outstretched arms taking regular selfies. And some museum officials agree that selfies can be a positive thing, as people often share their photos on social media sites, thereby generating free publicity for museums. It could also be argued that taking selfies helps people build lasting relationships with works of art, developing an appreciation of art that lasts beyond the initial visit and widening the appeal of art, especially for a younger generation.

Though no negative incidents linked to selfie sticks have yet been reported, many museums are taking preventative* measures just in case.

Glossary

scenario (noun) a particular situation or set of circumstances
preventative (adjective) designed to stop something bad before it can happen

3. **Read the words and phrases from the passage. Are they used to express a negative or positive opinion?**

   > agree   bad manners   complaining   distracting   free publicity   helps   miss out   negative incidents   positive   worry

Exam tip

Look out for positive and negative words in a passage which tell you about different opinions: *worry, negative, agree, help,* etc.

4. **What do you think about using selfie sticks in museums? Explain your opinion. Use the language below and the words in exercise 3.**

   > I (don't) think …   I (don't) believe …   I worry …   I agree / disagree …

5   **Read the passage below and answer the questions.**

     a) What is Vantablack?   **b)** Who invented it?   **c)** Who has the legal right to use it in art?

Can You Own a Colour?

One artist has exclusive rights to the world's blackest substance.

What's the blackest black on the planet? It's not the colour of coal, the midnight sky or even a panther's fur. The blackest shade on Earth actually comes from a human-made substance called Vantablack. It is believed to be the darkest material ever created, but that's not what has generated attention. Recently, sculptor Anish Kapoor bought the exclusive rights to use Vantablack in art. Now many are asking whether an artist should have a monopoly* on a material or colour.

Vantablack was originally developed by a British company called Surrey NanoSystems as a coating for military and scientific instruments. Nearly all the light that hits its surface is absorbed, making objects coated in the substance almost impossible to see. Some people say it's like looking into a hole. When asked about the artistic applications of the material,

Kapoor told the BBC, 'Imagine a space that is so dark that as you walk in you lose all sense of where you are, what you are, and especially all sense of time.'

Kapoor makes sculptures that explore form and space. Some people believe that he is the perfect person to experiment with Vantablack, but many in the art community object. They argue that, if Kapoor has sole access to Vantablack, he is preventing other artists from innovating with the new substance.

This isn't the first time an artist has claimed a colour for himself. In 1960, French conceptual artist Yves Klein created and patented his own vivid shade of blue. Kapoor didn't invent Vantablack, though, and it's not a paint colour but a unique substance. Representatives of Surrey NanoSystems say that as scientists, they're staying out of the discussion, stating, 'This debate is for the artistic community, we don't want to get involved.'

Glossary

monopoly (noun) a situation where only one person or company is able to use or to sell something

6   **Find the words and phrases (1–6) in the passage. Do they describe …**

     a) Arguments for Kapoor   **b)** Arguments against Kapoor   **c)** Neither side of the debate

1 asking whether … should _b_	**3** object	**5** staying out of the discussion ....
2 the perfect person	**4** they argue … preventing	**6** don't want to get involved ....

✏ EXAM TASK: Reading (identifying writer's views)

Exam tip

'Identifying writer's claims' questions focus on opinions expressed in a passage. If the opinion is not mentioned in the passage, then answer is *not given*.

7   **Do the following statements agree with the claims of the writer in the reading passage, *Can You Own a Colour*? Write:**

     YES   if the statement agrees with the information

     NO   if the statement contradicts the information

     NOT GIVEN   if there is no information about this in the passage

     1   Some people question whether giving one artist exclusive rights to use a colour is a good thing. ....

     2   Kapoor suggests Vantablack could be used to create artworks that offer the viewer a unique experience.

     3   Kapoor believes Vantablack is perfectly suited to his style of art. ....

     4   Some other artists oppose the idea that only Kapoor should be able to use Vantablack. ....

     5   The art community agreed that Yves Klein should have sole use of the colour he invented. ....

     6   The company who developed Vantablack publicly support Kapoor's use of it in his art. ....

Water worries

1 **Work in groups. Read the questions and brainstorm your ideas.**

- How many different ways do you use water in your everyday life?

- How could you reduce the amount of water you use every day?

2 **Read paragraph A of the passage. Answer the questions.**

a) Which place is the paragraph about?

b) What problem does it describe?

c) What are people doing to cope?

All dried up

A Brown grass, fewer toilet flushes and shorter showers. These are just some of the ways Californians are saving water as the state's water supply continues to shrink. With California experiencing its longest drought in 1,000 years, the governor issued mandatory* water restrictions in April. In cities like Los Angeles and San Francisco, people have cut back their water usage by 10 to 35 per cent by not watering lawns and using less in bathrooms and kitchens.

B Although the drought is forcing all Californians to change their habits, it's farmers who are really feeling the effects. California is the top US producer of more than 30 kinds of fruits, vegetables and nuts. Those crops require water, and lots of it. In fact, farms use half of the total water consumed in California.

C This isn't the first time that US farmers have had to cope with drought conditions. During the 1930s, a severe drought due to unusually low rainfall and higher-than-average temperatures caused huge dust storms across much of the central USA. The storms were so frequent that the region became known as the Dust Bowl.

D In the decade before the Dust Bowl, the government had encouraged farmers to move to the region. Settlers had ploughed up the prairie grass that naturally covered the area and planted wheat and other crops in its place. For a few years, their crops flourished, but then climate conditions changed and rainfall dropped. Native prairie grasses had evolved to withstand drought, but the wheat planted by farmers soon died. Ploughing the ground had also loosened the soil, so when the winds blew, huge clouds of dust were lifted up.

E Since the Dust Bowl region recovered in the early 1940s, agricultural practices have changed. Rather than relying on rainfall alone, farmers irrigate their fields by pumping up water stored in underground soil and rocks. But the region is once again in trouble.

F 'Everybody is trying to figure out what they're going to do,' says Ruben Arroyo, agriculture commissioner of Kern County, the state's leading producer of pistachios and grapes. Many farmers there have cut back on the area of land they're growing crops on: they planted 20,000 fewer acres this growing season.

G Reducing a farm's water use, though, is not easy for crops that grow on trees and vines, like almonds, walnuts or grapes. Not watering the trees or vines for a season could kill them and cause a loss of generations' worth of investment. It would also mean the loss of potential future crops.

H 'The drought is making people realise just how much water it takes to grow crops,' says Caitrin Phillips Chappelle, a researcher at the Public Policy Institute of California. Her organisation has been studying water usage in the state. Scientists estimate that 11 trillion gallons of water are needed for California to overcome the drought, which began in 2011. They say it may take years for the state to recover. Hopefully California will get more rain soon. Otherwise, residents may soon face even more water restrictions. 'We all just have to adjust our way of life,' says Chappelle.

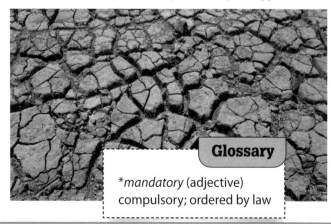

Glossary

mandatory (adjective) compulsory; ordered by law

3a Read the complete passage quickly. Which paragraphs are about:

a) the current situation? .... b) events in the past? ....

3b Work in pairs, A and B. Student A: find information in the passage about crops grown in the 1930s and problems farmers experienced at that time. Student B: find information about crops grown now and about problems that farmers are experiencing now.

3c Share your answers with your partner. What are the differences between the situation now and during the 1930s?

4 Match the actions to the reasons.

1 People have stopped watering their gardens. _a_

2 People are taking shorter showers ....

3 The introduction of water restrictions. ....

4 Using underground water to irrigate their crops. ....

5 Some farmers have planted fewer crops. ....

6 Farmers need to keep watering vines and trees. ....

a) To reduce water usage

b) To avoid losing a valuable investment

c) To reduce their dependence on water from rain

5 Complete the statements about the passage using words or phrases from the box.

caused   could cause   due to   ~~effects~~   mean   rather than

a) The ....._effects_..... of the current drought have been most serious for farmers.

b) The 1930s drought was .... unusually dry and hot weather conditions.

c) Farmers now use water from underground sources .... just relying on rain.

d) If trees or vines die, it .... farmers to lose many years of investment.

6a Read and underline the key words in the questions in exercise 6b. Do not look at the answers yet. Note down which paragraph of the passage you think the answer will be in.

✎ EXAM TASK: Reading (multiple choice questions)

6b Now answer the questions. Circle the correct letter, A, B, or C.

1 How have Californian residents reduced their water usage?

　A By growing fewer crops

　B By using water from underground sources

　C By using less water in their homes

2 What caused the drought during the 1930s?

　A A period of unusually hot, dry weather

　B The removal of naturally growing prairie grass

　C Ploughing the soil to grow crops

3 Why did farmers in the Dust Bowl region start to water their crops from underground sources?

　A To make them grow more strongly

　B To reduce their reliance on rainfall

　C To reduce their water usage

4 Why do farmers have to continue watering crops that grow on vines and trees?

　A Because almonds, walnuts and grapes are very profitable

　B Because vines and trees continue to produce crops over many years

　C Because vines and trees are more vulnerable to dry conditions

5 What does Chappelle think people may have to do in the future?

　A Change the way they use water

　B Do more research into water usage.

　C Find new sources of water.

Helpful microbes

1a Work in groups of four. Two students read text A and two students read text B. Answer the questions.

a) What substance is the text about?   **b)** What is it used for?

Text A
Penicillin is a common type of antibiotic drug which is used widely in medicine to treat infections. Penicillin is actually a type of mould that grows naturally.
It works by attacking the bacteria which cause infections and stopping them from spreading.

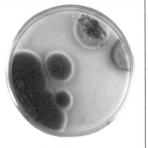

Text B
Yeast is a tiny organism, actually a type of fungus, which has been used in baking for thousands of years. In foods such as bread, the yeast is mixed with flour, salt and warm water or milk.
The yeast produces carbon dioxide, which creates bubbles in the dough and makes it swell.

1b In your groups, describe the substance you read about. Try to use your own words.

2 Read the main passage. Copy and complete the table below with information from the passage.

Places where microbes are found on / in the human body	The health benefits of microbes
skin	help to digest foods, e.g. fibre

The bugs on us

A If you take a close look at your arm, you'll see skin, pores and arm hair. But what if you magnified this view 1,000 times? You'd see more than a million bacteria, fungi and other tiny creatures on a single square centimetre of skin. And it's not just on your arm; the human body is teeming with 100 trillion microbes, or microscopic organisms. In all, these microbes outnumber the body's own cells by a ratio of 10 to 1.

B It may sound unpleasant, but it's a good thing you're covered head to toe in microbes. Most of them are harmless hitchhikers feeding on sweat, skin oils and food as it digests in the stomach, while many are also important for human health. Collectively, all these creatures make up what is known as the human microbiome.

C Until recently, we didn't know exactly kinds of microbes lived on the human body or what they all did. Since 2007, scientists working on the Human Microbiome Project have identified more than 10,000 different microbial species that live on and inside the human body. Not only is there great variety, but each species finds particular spots on the body where conditions are just right for them.

D Microbes live on every part of the body that is exposed to air, including the lungs and stomach. Since each body part has a specific ecosystem, microbes have created various niches for themselves. Similar bacteria live in damp places like armpits and behind the knees. Nostrils are home to viruses that infect the bacteria living there. About 80 types of fungi live on your heels. Mites nestle in eyelashes, eating dead skin and oil. However, even places with similar conditions can have drastically different resident microbes. The roof of your mouth is covered in different bacteria from your teeth. Your left hand's microbes are different from those on your right hand, depending on which hand you use more often.

E Our microbiome keeps us healthy, says Pat Schloss, a microbiologist at the University of Michigan. 'We eat a lot of foods that our body can't digest on its own. We need bacteria in our guts to break down things like fibre.' Even E. Coli, the bacteria that cause food poisoning, are vital to our bodies, as long as they stay in the lower intestine.

F Working with the immune system, microbes are often the first line of defence against invading germs, as they fight to protect their space on our bodies. Based on what we are learning from the Human Microbiome Project, doctors are turning to microbes to fight infections.

G This raises the question though, of why our immune systems don't fight off these friendly microbes. Between birth and age three, our immune system and microbiome develop together. Thus the immune system recognises our microbes as just another part of us.

H An individual's microbiome is so unique that it's like a fingerprint. People living in the same house have similar microbiomes, but not classmates, friends or colleagues. Even though you might spend every day with someone at school, at university or at work, you won't exchange as many microbes with friends and colleagues as you do with family members.

3 A *microbe* is a tiny (microscopic) organism. Which of the words in the box are examples of microbes mentioned in the passage?

> bacteria   L. Coli   fibre   fungi   infection   mite   niche   virus   vitamin

4 Underline another word or phrase in the passage which refers to the same thing as the word(s) a–g in the passage.

a) (paragraph A) these microbes

b) (paragraph B) Most of them

c) (paragraph B) all these creatures

d) (paragraph C) each species

e) (paragraph E) They

f) (paragraph F) they

g) (paragraph H) family members

5a Read the sentence from paragraph A. What does *outnumber* mean? Are there more of the microbes or more of the body's own cells?

(paragraph A) In all, these microbes <u>outnumber</u> the body's own cells by a ratio of 10 to 1.

5b Read the multiple choice question below. Choose the option, A–D, which makes a statement with the same meaning as the passage.

The human body has ten times …

A the number of bacteria compared to its own cells.

B more human cells than bacteria, fungi and other microbes.

C as many bacteria, fungi and other microscopic organisms as its own cells.

D more microbes than other microscopic creatures.

✎ EXAM TASK: Reading (multiple choice questions)

6 Answer the questions. Choose the correct letter, A, B, C or D.

1 The human microbiome consists of …

A many different types of microbes that live on and in the body.

B those microbes that are essential to stay healthy.

C microbes which feed on the body without causing any harm.

D tiny creatures that live on the skin.

2 Before 2007, scientists …

A didn't know that microbes lived on and inside the human body.

B had identified 10,000 different microbes, but didn't understand their function.

C didn't have detailed evidence about the exact number and function of microbes.

D didn't know that microbes lived inside the lungs and stomach.

3 Different types of microbes …

A are found in the armpits and behind the knees.

B can exist with or without exposure to air.

C exploit the conditions that exist in different parts of the body.

D create special ecosystems on the right and left side of the body.

4 Each person's individual microbiome …

A can be identified using their fingerprint.

B shares features with those of their close relatives.

C is similar to that of their family, friends and workmates.

D does not change through their lifetime.

Chocolate catastrophe?

coffee berries

ginger root

cocoa pod

1   **Work in groups. Discuss how and where the plants in the photographs are grown and how they are used in food and drink.**

2a   **Work in pairs. Read the passage. Some pairs follow the instructions for A and some for B.**

Pair A: Which people and groups:	**Pair B:** Make notes on:
a) Are mentioned more than once?	a) The causes of the chocolate shortage
b) Feel negative or positive about the situation?	b) The effects on people and the environment
	c) Possible solutions

2b   **Work with another pair who answered different questions (A or B). Share your answers.**

Is Chocolate Disappearing?

A The world is in the midst of a chocolate shortage, and chocolate makers say it could get worse. According to Mars Inc. and Barry Callebaut, two of the world's largest chocolate manufacturers, people are eating more cocoa than farmers can grow. Last year, globally, people ate 70,000 tons more cocoa than was produced. Chocolate makers say that deficit could reach 1 million tons by 2020 and 2 million tons by 2030.

B Most of the world's cocoa is grown in Africa. Cocoa trees bear bright fruit pods that each contain 30 to 50 cocoa seeds. These seeds are removed from the pods and left to ferment* for several days, a process that produces the distinctive chocolate flavour. The seeds are then dried and roasted, and the shells are removed to reveal the cocoa nib inside. Finally, the nibs are ground and mixed with sugar, vanilla and sometimes milk to create the final product: a bar of dark, milk or white chocolate.

C High temperatures and dry weather in West Africa have greatly hurt production. Growers and chocolate makers are also concerned about the increase in plant diseases that are destroying crops. The International Cocoa Organization (ICCO) estimates that one such disease, known as 'frosty pod' (a type of fungal infection), has reduced world cocoa production by 30 to 40 per cent.

D To try to grow more chocolate, farmers are converting diverse tropical forest to cocoa farms, says Peter Läderach, a scientist with the International Centre for Tropical Agriculture in Vietnam. This expansion is destroying large areas of the Guinean Rainforest. The area has been identified as a biodiversity hotspot with a high concentration of plant and animal species which are being threatened. The slash and burn* technique used by farmers not only destroys the forest, leaving the soil infertile, but also forces wildlife into smaller and smaller areas.

E Another factor contributing to the deficit is the rapidly increasing demand for chocolate. People in China ate 40,000 tons of chocolate in 2010, and are expected to consume 70,000 tons this year. India's chocolate consumption is projected to rise from 25,000 tons in 2010 to 40,000 this year.

F As cocoa prices continue to rise, confectionery companies may produce smaller bars in an attempt to conserve cocoa. Farmers have been producing a new strain* of cacao, the seed from which cocoa is made, called CCN-51. This strain is resistant to some of the diseases affecting cocoa production, and it produces about seven times more cocoa beans than typical cocoa strains, but its taste is less flavourful.

G The picture isn't completely pessimistic, though. One Central American research organisation has developed more new strains of cacao that are disease-resistant but still taste good. Läderach also points out that if current climate warming patterns continue, cocoa could be grown in areas of the world where it wasn't possible before.

H And some experts believe reports of the shortage have been exaggerated. 'While our projections show that supply deficits are likely to occur in the next several years,' the ICCO said in a statement, 'stocks of cocoa beans should cushion this development before production growth accelerates.' So the world's chocolate lovers may not need to panic just yet.

Glossary

*ferment (verb) when a substance ferments, chemical changes happen to it
*slash and burn (noun) when people cut down trees and burn the area to clear the land for farming
*strain (noun) a particular type of a plant

3a Work in pairs. Find examples in the passage of:

a) people or groups that disagree

b) criticisms

c) predictions

Exam tip

It is important to recognise who says what in a passage in order to answer the questions. Sometimes a person or group is named: *According to Mars Inc. …., the ICCO said …..* Where no person or group is mentioned, the views are those of the writer.

3b Identify who in the passage:

a) has different opinions

b) is criticising

c) made the predictions

Exam tip

Read the instructions for multiple-choice questions carefully. Sometimes you need to choose only one answer, sometimes you need to select two or three correct answers for each question.

4 Read the exam questions in exercises 5 and 6 below. Answer the questions.

a) How many options are there for each question? ....

b) How many answers do you need to choose? ....

✎ EXAM TASK: Reading (multiple choice questions)

5 Choose TWO correct answers.

1 On what points do chocolate makers agree with the ICCO?

A The cocoa deficit is likely to get much worse in the future.

B Consumers are buying more chocolate than is currently being produced.

C There are enough stocks of cocoa that chocolate production won't be significantly affected.

D Cocoa production has been badly affected in recent years by diseases.

E Chocolate bars are likely to decrease in size and quality.

2 What criticisms does the writer make of cocoa farming methods in West Africa?

A The cocoa is of low quality and has less flavour

B Land clearance is destroying important areas of rainforest

C Farmers are not being paid fairly for their crops

D Wildlife is suffering as a result of habitat loss caused by farming

E The climate is not suitable for growing cocoa

6 Choose THREE correct answers.

1 Which factors does the writer mention that have led to the cocoa shortage?

A New strains of cocoa have less flavour

B Demand for chocolate globally has increased

C The main cocoa-producing area has experienced drought conditions

D Farmers are destroying rainforest areas to grow more cocoa

E Cocoa crops have been seriously affected by disease

F Cocoa production in South America and Asia has declined

G There are no stocks of cocoa for suppliers to sell

2 Which options does the writer mention that might help increase cocoa production?

A New farming methods that use less land to grow crops

B New pesticides to control diseases that affect cocoa trees

C Cocoa could be grown in new parts of the world as the climate warms.

D Increasing production in Asia and South America

E New strains of cacao that can produce more cocoa

F Chocolate products could be developed with a lower cocoa content

G New strains of cacao which are less susceptible to disease

READING PASSAGE 1

Massive meltdown

A This past July, Brandon Overstreet stood at the edge of a brilliant blue river winding across a vast glacier, known as an ice sheet, in Greenland. The rushing water at his feet was only a degree above freezing – a result of massive amounts of ice melting. Just downstream the river fell into a moulin, a vertical waterfall within the ice sheet. Overstreet carried a bag with 23 metres of rope inside. His mission: to throw the bag across the river to scientists on the other side. One wrong step and he would be swept to his death by the cold water. For Overstreet and his team, the dangerous work is worth it: they're trying to understand how a warming world is melting Greenland's ice – and how coastal communities could be affected by the additional water flowing into the world's oceans.

B Eighty per cent of Greenland is covered by an ice sheet. In the 1970s, NASA started taking photos of Earth from satellites in orbit. The images taken over 45 years show that the Earth's glaciers, including those in Greenland, are shrinking dramatically. A recent study by scientists from the University of Copenhagen in Denmark found that from 2003 to 2010, ice on the Greenland ice sheet melted more than twice as quickly as it did during the 20th century.

C Scientists have concluded that this melting is mainly due to climate change. About 8,000 years ago, human activity began to alter Earth's climate says Richard Williams, a geologist at the Stefánsson Arctic Institute in Iceland. Cutting down trees and burning coal for fuel have released greenhouse gases, such as carbon dioxide, into the atmosphere. These gases act like a blanket around Earth, trapping energy that warms the planet. As the temperature rises, Earth's glacier ice melts and meltwater flows into the oceans, raising the level of the seas.

D The Intergovernmental Panel on Climate Change estimates that ice melt will raise sea levels by one metre by 2100. This estimate comes from surveys that scientists have taken to reveal how much ice is melting, and how quickly. The data also suggest that there's enough ice in the Greenland ice sheet alone to raise the world's sea levels by seven metres if all of it were to melt. Since Greenland's temperatures remain around freezing, an increase of just a few degrees creates ideal melting conditions – a scenario that greatly concerns scientists.

E 'In a low-lying area, one foot of sea level rise can translate to a quarter mile of flooding inland,' says Williams. 'You can go to Miami, Florida, to see it happening,' he says. There, the level of the sea is rising by almost an inch a year. Seawater is creeping towards beachfront homes, flooding roads and contaminating drinking wells with salt. As seas rise, people living in Miami and other coastal communities will have to be relocated. 'We need to start planning now,' says Williams.

F That's where Overstreet's mission comes in. He's a graduate student in hydrology (the study of water) at the University of Wyoming and part of a team of scientists studying Greenland's ice. By throwing his bag across the river, he enabled the scientists to set up a cable over it. They then attached a small, specially designed surfboard to it, which floated on the river. The board was equipped with instruments to measure the river's depth, width, temperature and rate of flow. This allowed the team to track precisely how fast the ice was melting.

G The data the team collected confirmed that models do a really good job of predicting ice loss. 'It was immediately apparent how connected meltwater production is to temperature,' says Overstreet. Before sunrise, about six cubic metres (1,600 gallons) of meltwater flowed through the river per second. But once the day warmed up, that increased to as much as 24 cubic metres (6,300 gallons) – enough water rushing by each second to fill about 85 bathtubs. A worrying amount, and one of the reasons why the scientists continue the risky work of monitoring the meltwaters. 'It's hard, dangerous work,' says Overstreet, 'but we're out there because we're passionate about understanding climate change.'

Questions 1–7

Reading Passage 1 has seven sections, **A–G**.

Which section contains the following information?

Write the correct letter, **A–G** in boxes **1–7**.

---

1 A way of collecting the necessary data on ice melt.

2 The cause of the melt problem.

3 A prediction of how much ice melt will affect sea levels.

4 A way that the speed of ice melt has been recorded.

5 A way that specific weather affects research results.

6 A risk taken to get the research done.

7 The impact of ice melt on urban life.

Questions 8–10

Do the following statements agree with the information given in Reading Passage 1?

In boxes **8–10** on your answer sheet, write:

TRUE   if the statement agrees with the information

FALSE   if the statement contradicts the information

NOT GIVEN   if there is no information on this

---

8 If Greenland's ice sheet melts completely, it will raise sea levels by seven metres.

9 Climate change cannot be blamed entirely on human activity.

10 Flooding in some coastal areas results in an increase in the sea level.

Questions 11–14

Label the diagram below.

Choose **ONE WORD ONLY** from the passage for each answer.

Write your answers in gaps **11–14**.

Greenland's Ice Sheet

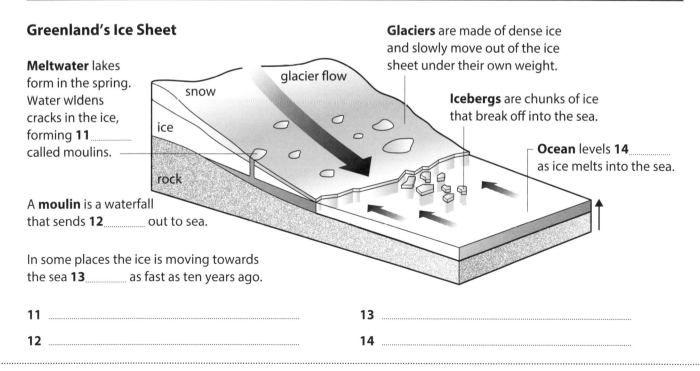

Meltwater lakes form in the spring. Water widens cracks in the ice, forming **11**............ called moulins.

snow

glacier flow

ice

rock

Glaciers are made of dense ice and slowly move out of the ice sheet under their own weight.

Icebergs are chunks of ice that break off into the sea.

Ocean levels **14**............ as ice melts into the sea.

A **moulin** is a waterfall that sends **12**............ out to sea.

In some places the ice is moving towards the sea **13**............ as fast as ten years ago.

11 ....

12 ....

13 ....

14 ....

READING PASSAGE 2

Is screen time making you sick?

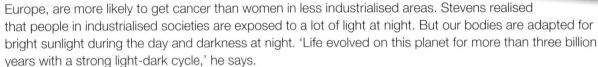

A Whether you're texting friends, spending time online or watching TV, you probably stare at a bright screen before going to bed. If so, you may want to rethink your evening routine: scientists believe that night-time exposure to the light from these devices can disrupt your body's natural rhythms. It may even give you cancer. Luckily, you can take steps to protect yourself.

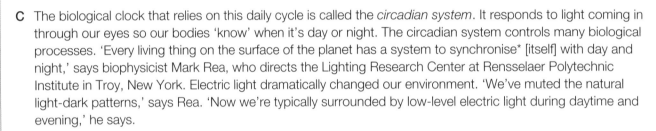

B Richard Stevens, a scientist at the University of Connecticut who studies cancer, first suggested a link between light and health in the 1980s. He was trying to understand why women in industrialised regions, like North America and Western Europe, are more likely to get cancer than women in less industrialised areas. Stevens realised that people in industrialised societies are exposed to a lot of light at night. But our bodies are adapted for bright sunlight during the day and darkness at night. 'Life evolved on this planet for more than three billion years with a strong light-dark cycle,' he says.

C The biological clock that relies on this daily cycle is called the *circadian system*. It responds to light coming in through our eyes so our bodies 'know' when it's day or night. The circadian system controls many biological processes. 'Every living thing on the surface of the planet has a system to synchronise* [itself] with day and night,' says biophysicist Mark Rea, who directs the Lighting Research Center at Rensselaer Polytechnic Institute in Troy, New York. Electric light dramatically changed our environment. 'We've muted the natural light-dark patterns,' says Rea. 'Now we're typically surrounded by low-level electric light during daytime and evening,' he says.

D To understand how light might affect health, Stevens asked other scientists if they knew of any biological effects of light on animals in scientific laboratories. One mentioned that light exposure at the wrong time of day reduces the amount of the hormone melatonin in animals' bodies. People normally produce melatonin in the evening as part of their natural circadian rhythm to make them sleepy. The news that light affects melatonin levels caught Stevens's attention. Earlier studies had shown that melatonin helps protects against cancerous tumours. Stevens realised that if light at night reduces melatonin, and melatonin prevents cancer, then night-time light could increase cancer rates.

E Stevens and others decided that they could test this through observations. For example, if seeing light at night contributes to cancer, then blind people should get cancer less often than sighted people, people who work night shifts should get it more often than those who work during the day, and cancer rates should be higher in areas with more electric light on at night. Studies provide support for all of these theories. The evidence was strong enough that, in 2007, the World Health Organization declared night-shift work to be a 'probable carcinogen', meaning it probably causes cancer.

F However, not all light affects our body clock equally: 'The circadian system is basically a blue-sky detector,' says Rea. 'It's looking for short-wavelength blue light.' Blue light keeps us awake and prevents melatonin production. Sunlight contains all colours, including blue, so it's a clear signal for daytime, but seeing white fluorescent lights or glowing screens at night can fool our circadian system into thinking it's day. 'Our modern devices – phones, laptops, iPads – they're all rich in blue light,' says Anne-Marie Chang, a neuroscientist at Penn State University. Chang recently led a study comparing reading on an iPad versus a printed book before bed. She found that people reading iPads produced less melatonin in the evening, took longer to fall asleep and felt less alert the next morning.

G The good news is that you can protect yourself: the best idea is to get some exposure to bright light in the morning and avoid glowing screens at night. If you need to use a device at night, adjust the screen so it is not too bright. Some computer apps change the screens automatically so that they produce less blue light at night. Small changes like these can help keep your body running like clockwork.

> **Glossary**
>
> *synchronise* to occur at the same rate or time as something else

Questions 1–4

Reading Passage 2 has seven paragraphs, **A–G**.

Which section contains the following information? Write the correct letter, **A–G**, in boxes **1–4**.

NB You may use any letter more than once.

1 proof that a theory was correct

2 the reason for the initial research

3 help from scientists in other fields

4 a warning given by an international institution

Questions 5–8

Look at the following statements (Questions 5–8) and the list of people below.

Match each statement with the correct person, **A–C**.

Write the correct letter, **A–C**, in boxes **5–8**. You can use the letters more than once.

5 Screens produce one particular type of light.

6 The distinction between day and night is not so clear these days.

7 Looking at screens at night could increase the risk of getting cancer.

8 People who read books on devices take longer to fall asleep.

List of People

A Mark Rea

B Anne-Marie Chang

C Richard Stevens

Questions 9–13

Complete the summary below.

Choose **NO MORE THAN TWO WORDS** from the passage for each answer.

Write your answers in boxes **9–13**.

Human beings have a circadian rhythm that relies on day and night.

In the evening, when there is an absence of light, humans produce a hormone called melatonin that makes them feel **9** .... Melatonin also protects the body from **10** ....

These days many people use devices that produce light before they go to bed. Studies have found that exposure to these devices make people fall asleep later. In addition, people who use these devices late at night don't feel as **11** .... in the mornings.

Scientists advise people to **12** .... using devices at night. But if you have to use them, you shouldn't make the **13** .... very bright.

READING PASSAGE 3

Save the bees

Honeybees do some amazing jobs that make our lives a lot sweeter. Not only do they produce honey, but they also pollinate many important crops, including apples, pears and almonds.

But these insects are facing tough times. In 2015, beekeepers in the USA reported that more than 40 per cent of their honeybee colonies (the group of bees that live together in a hive) had died over the previous 12 months. The bad news came after several hard years for honeybees. Today, scientists are working on understanding why bees are struggling – and what can be done to help them.

In the USA, beekeepers manage 2.7 million colonies of honeybees. Farmers often pay for pollination services from beekeepers, who pack their colonies onto trucks and travel from farm to farm.

Around 2005, beekeepers began to notice that something was wrong with their honeybees. For several years, about a third of US honeybee colonies were lost every winter. Adult worker bees, which are the females that gather pollen, disappeared. They left behind their queen bee and the unhatched brood (developing young). Without the worker bees to provide food, the whole colony often died. Researchers named this Colony Collapse Disorder (CCD).

In 2011, scientists launched a nationwide programme, called the Bee Informed Partnership, to collect and analyse data from beekeepers on how many of their colonies were lost each year. 'We can't go out and look at all the bees,' says bee researcher Jeffrey Pettis of the US Department of Agriculture (USDA). 'So the beekeepers report losses and symptoms to us, and we can get a picture of bee health.'

It's still not clear exactly what causes CCD, but many scientists believe it is a combination of things, including parasites (the insects or mites that live on bees), poor diet and pesticides (the chemicals used on crops).

In the past few years, the surveys have shown some surprising and concerning results. 'We've started seeing fewer classic cases of CCD,' says Pettis, 'but we're still seeing high losses every year. It's not that the worker bees are all disappearing the way they used to. We're seeing colonies get weak and die first. Sometimes the queen dies and isn't replaced. Sometimes bees seem to be dying of starvation.'

Additionally, the 2014–15 survey showed more summer deaths than winter ones. 'This is unheard of,' says bee scientist, and Bee Informed Partnership project director, Dennis vanEngelsdorp, of the University of Maryland.

Although the pattern of colony deaths has changed, the likely causes of CCD are still to blame in the current wave of honeybee losses. 'We think things like parasite mites, poor diet and pesticide exposure are taking a toll,' says Pettis. 'In any given year, one might be worse than another.'

One parasite, called the varroa mite, has been especially troublesome. The mites attach to bees' bodies and suck out their blood, which weakens the bees. They also spread viruses that make bees sick.

Pesticides become a problem when farmers use them on crops to control insects that might eat their plants. When honeybees arrive to pollinate, they're exposed to the harmful chemicals.

Another problem for some honeybee colonies is their diet. Sometimes farmers hire beekeepers to have their bees pollinate huge fields of a single crop. 'Bees need good nutrition to stay healthy, and we think sometimes if they're only gathering nectar and pollen from one crop, they may not be getting all the nutrients they need,' says Pettis.

The USDA is trying to solve the problem of the bees' poor diet through a number of programmes, such as offering farmers money to grow beneficial plants on their land and to grow wildflowers among their crops.

Beekeepers are also being encouraged to treat varroa mite infections. 'Mite control is at the top of our list of ways we think we can make a difference in saving bees,' says vanEngelsdorp.

Homeowners can tackle the problem too, says Pettis. 'Grow pollinator-friendly plants in your yard,' he says, 'and minimise the use of pesticides.' After all, helping honeybees has big benefits. 'If you like fruits, nuts and vegetables,' says Pettis, 'all of those are pollinated by honeybees.'

Questions 1–4

Choose the correct letter, **A**, **B**, **C** or **D**.

Write the correct letter in boxes **1–4**.

1 What is the initial cause of Colony Collapse Disorder?

   A The unhatched colony brood die in the winter.

   B The worker bees from a colony fail to return to the hive.

   C The pollen available is insufficient to feed the colony.

   D The queen leaves the colony in search of food and does not return.

2 Why was the Bee Informed Partnership established?

   A To take photographs of colonies with common symptoms.

   B To present data on bees to the US Department of Agriculture (USDA).

   C To visit beekeepers with specific problems.

   D To gather data on bees from different parts of the USA.

3 What surprising result did a recent survey on US bee health show?

   A Bees were dying during a different time period.

   B Some bees were quickly recovering from illnesses.

   C Bee deaths were higher than expected.

   D Bees were adapting well to colder weather.

4 How can the general public help bees?

   A By eating more fruit, vegetables and nuts.

   B By asking farmers to stop using pesticides.

   C By growing flowers that are good for bees.

   D By looking out for bees with infections.

Questions 5–9

Which five of the following claims about bees are made in the passage? Choose **FIVE** letters, **A–J**.

Write the correct letters in boxes **5–9**.

A Bees are getting used to the chemicals farmers use.

B Bee deaths are caused by a number of factors.

C Some wild plants in fields can be harmful to bees.

D Bees need a varied diet to stay healthy.

E Bee deaths are sometimes caused by a lack of food.

F Bee deaths are mainly caused by the varroa mite.

G Farmers are being encouraged to help solve the problem.

H Honey bees are less likely to pollinate certain crops.

I Killing the varroa mite is a priority for scientists.

J The amount of honey being produced in the USA is decreasing.

Questions 10–13

Answer the questions below.

Choose **NO MORE THAN TWO WORDS AND / OR A NUMBER** from the passage for each answer.

Write the correct words and / or numbers in boxes **10–13**.

10 Which two types of fruit mentioned in the article do honeybees pollinate?

11 How many honeybee colonies are there in the USA?

12 How do beekeepers transport their colonies to different places?

13 In 2005, what proportion of honeybee colonies died every winter?

Answers

Lighting the Olympic flame (pages 6–7)

1   Students' own answers.

2   **b)** Berlin, Beijing **c)** 1982, 1780 **d)** four years, 20 metres
e) doctor, poet **f)** iron, gold **g)** dangerous, too expensive
h) educational, tourist attraction

How long can have two different meanings;
a measurement, or a length of time.

3a   **1 Suggested underlining:** modern
2 Suggested underlining: first

3b   Students' own answers.

4a   **section A:** Athens, 20th century, Amsterdam, 1928
section B: 1936, Berlin

4b   **1** Amsterdam **2** 1936

4c   **5** worldwide **6** (by a) woman

5   **3** sunlight **4** (by) plane **5** 78 days **6** 1968 **7** prince
8 204 **9** too heavy **10** magnesium

6   Students' own answers.

7   **a)** B **b)** A

Cities of the future (pages 8–9)

1a–b Students' own answers.

2a   carrot, onion, potato

2b   **Key word:** currently; **Correct answer:** potato

3   **a)** five years **b)** submarine

4   Students' own answers.

5   **1** Radio stations **2** storm **3** spherical **4** methane **5** resin
6 bridges
7 tourist attraction **8** waves **9** rain

6   **b)** give up **c)** generate **d)** provide **e)** form
f) supply

7   **b)** supply food **c)** provide housing
d) established a settlement **e)** give up the idea
f) generate electricity

Diamonds are forever (pages 10–11)

1a   **a)** False. Diamonds can be many colours including yellow,
blue, green and pink. These are sometimes more valuable
than clear diamonds. **b)** True **c)** False. It is possible to
produce artificial diamonds by putting carbon under a
high temperature and high pressure. It is also possible to
grow them in the laboratory using a carbon gas mixture.

d) True. They also referred to them as 'Tears of the gods'.

1b   Students' own answers.

2a–b Students' own answers. The easiest words to see are
probably *2014* because the numbers are easy to see
against the rest of the passage, '*Mountain of Light*',
because you can look for the quotation marks and *Queen
Victoria* because you can look for the capital letters.

3   **b)** one of the rarest shades (different words)

c) the largest clear diamond in the world (change from
comparative to superlative expression)

d) unaware of its value (different words)

e) diamonds were discovered in Brazil by prospectors
(change from active to passive)

4   Students' own answers.

5a   **2** A **3** D **4** F **5** B **6** C

5b   **2** A **3** E **4** C **5** D **6** B

6   **b)** theft **c)** exotic **d)** unaware **e)** boom **f)** auction

Healthy choices (pages 12–13)

1a–b Students' own answers.

2   **b)** 4, 5 **c)** 3, 5

3   Students' own answers.

4a   Brian Wansink, Jo Bartel, Dr Julianna Van der Pluym,
Dr Craig Canapari, Dr Douglas Lazzaro

4b   **b)** Jo Bartel **c)** Dr Julianna Van der Pluym **d)** Dr Craig
Canapari **e)** Brian Wansink

5a   **2** F **3** A **4** B **5** D **6** G **7** E

5b   **2** found **3** explain **4** recommend **5** advise
6 According to **7** suggest

6   **2** F **3** E **4** B **5** D **6** A

Mapping the world (pages 14–15)

1   Students' own answers.

2   **Suggested answers:**
a) The Grand Canyon in Arizona, USA
b) To record photos of the canyon
c) Views around the canyon
d) A special camera that someone can wear on a backpack

3a   **Suggested answer:**
Google recorded views of the Grand Canyon for Google
Maps.

3b Heading 2

4a Liwa Oasis, UAE; Bhutan; the Arctic; Barcelona; Paris; the White House; the Grand Canyon; the pyramids in Egypt

4b **Suggested answers:**
   a) Trekker: Liwa Oasis; the Arctic; Grand Canyon; Egyptian pyramids
   Trike: Barcelona; Paris
   Trolley: White House
   b) No roads so cars can't go there, narrow lanes, alleyways and doorways
   c) Mainly about the types of cameras

4c Students' own answers.

5 **b)** the background **c)** a design solution **d)** a context

6a Students' own answers.

6b A iv B ii C v D vii E iii

7 **b)** image **c)** site/spot **d)** site/spot **e)** capture
   f) photograph **g)** gather **h)** indoors

Connections (pages 16–17)

1 **Suggested answers:**
   a) between 1996 and 2005 – as the internet became popular, lots of cables were needed to create the basic network
   b) fishing: fishermen's nets and lines get caught on the cables

2a **Suggested answers:** railway lines, airports, ports, bus stops, bus stations

2b **a)** mobile phone towers, cables and other structures
   b) Internet infrastructure

3 **a)** A natural disasters, e.g. hurricanes; B earthquakes, coral reefs, sunken ships, anchors, fishermen's nets
   b) Between Tokyo and London across the Arctic
   c) Faster communication between London and Tokyo; the first fibre optic connection for Alaska and northern Canada

4 **Suggested answers:**
   a) to make a pattern of lines that cross each other
   b) (adjective) – that cannot be broken or damaged
   c) (adjective) – possible to be damaged
   d) (adjective) – likely to suffer something
   e) (noun) – objects that are in your way
   f) (noun)   a narrow route that you can pass through

5 **1** Internet infrastructure keeps our communications flowing, but it isn't invincible. It's vulnerable to threats like natural disasters.
   General idea: internet infrastructure can be damaged
   Specific idea: example of one type of damage – from natural disasters

2 New connections are being added all the time, both on land and at sea. Installing a cable at sea is a massive undertaking.
   General idea: new internet connections are being added
   Specific idea: details about adding one type of connection – at sea

3 One project aims to take advantage of climate change. Melting sea ice in the Arctic has opened up a new passageway between Asia and Europe.
   General idea: a project taking advantage of climate change
   Specific idea: the particular aspect of climate change – melting sea ice

6 A iii B ii C vii D v E i

Survival is in the eyes (pages 18–19)

1 Students' own answers.

2a **Animals:** cats, goats, sheep, deer, horses, big cats, wolves, bears

2b **Predators:** cats, big cats, wolves, bears
   Prey: goats, sheep, deer, horses

3a **Suggested answers:**
   A students:
   a) vertical
   b) It helps them to judge distance (so they can pounce on their prey)

   B students:
   a) horizontal
   b) They have a wider view around them to watch for predators and it's the best shape to see ahead to run away (for animals with eyes on the sides of their head)

3b Students' own answers.

4 **Section A** both **Section B** both **Section C** predators **Section D** predators **Section E** prey **Section F** man

5 **b)** vision **c)** predators **d)** simulated **e)** potential

6a–b Best heading = 2 – this section asks questions about <u>why</u> pupil shapes are different ('variation')
   Heading 1: the section mentions human and animal pupil shapes, but it is not the main idea
   Heading 3: researchers already know <u>how</u> pupil shape varies (some have vertical pupils, some horizontal) – the research wants to find out <u>why</u>

7 B v C i D viii E iii

Endangered and extinct (pages 20–21)

1   Students' own answers. In danger of extinction (suggested answers): rhinos, elephants, tigers, pandas

2   **a)** the passenger pigeon **b)** North America (USA and Canada) **c)** hunting **d)** (September 1) 1914 **e)** Students' own answers

3   **b)** arrival **c)** commercialise(d) **d)** construction **e)** invention **f)** movement **g)** loss **h)** disappearance

4a **b)** A, F **c)** B, D **d)** E, G

4b Students' own answers.

5a Students' own answers.

5b Questions 3 and 6

6   2 D 3 A 4 C 5 E 6 A

Firestorm (pages 22–23)

1   Students' own answers.

2   **Factor 2** fuel; Picture A **Factor 3** ignition; Picture B

3   **a)** and **c)**

4a **b)** risk **c)** cause **d)** effect

4b **Suggested answers:**
   a) more than 5 million acres of forest burned, thousands of people were evacuated from their homes
   b) lightning, campfires
   c) new trees can grow
   d) Africa
   e) high temperatures, low humidity, rain-free days, high winds

5a 1 severe fire seasons 2 forest ecosystem 3 global wildfire trends 4 common ways 5 wildfire trends 6 longer fire seasons

5b 2 D 3 G 4 C 5 F

Portrait of Venus (pages 24–25)

1   **a)** Neptune (not Pluto, as astronomers have now decided that Pluto is not a true planet) **b)** Jupiter / Mercury / Mars **c)** Saturn **d)** Earth **e)** Venus

2   **b)** uncountable noun **c)** plural noun **d)** uncountable noun **e)** singular noun

3   **b)** hydrogen **c)** moons **d)** iron **e)** centre

4   **b)** A **c)** B **d)** B **e)** A

5   **b)** mountain **c)** dust storms **d)** rings **e)** volcanic activity

6   Suggested underlining (not all sentences have words that are underlined): *Beginning / end of the day*, *active* and *clouds* could be scanning words for 1, 7 and 8, but you might find slightly different language in the text.
   2 Phosphorus, Hesperus 3 Galileo 4 1961 5 Magellan probe 6 Before the 1960s 9 billions of years ago

7   2 philosopher 3 phases 4 radar 5 density 6 rainforest 7 volcanoes 8 lightning 9 water

Citrus greening (pages 26–27)

1a

Crop	Top producer
tea	China
olive oil	Spain
cocoa	Ivory Coast
soya beans	USA
coconuts	Indonesia
oranges	Brazil

1b Students' own answers

2   **b)** ✓ **c)** ✓ **d)** ✗ **e)** ✗ **f)** ✓

3   Suggested underlining: **3** food and water system **4** veins **5** shaped, taste

4   **A:** after that, eventually
   B: as a result, in consequence, therefore

5   **a)** roots **b)** sugars **c)** yellow **d)** irregular **e)** bitter

6   Students' own answers

7   2 pesticide 3 wasp 4 advertising 5 proteins 6 consumers

People of the Tenere desert (pages 28–29)

1a/b Students' own answers

2   **b)** ✓ A **c)** not mentioned **d)** ✓ B, C **e)** ✓ B **f)** ✓ C, D, E **g)** not mentioned **h)** ✓ E

3a Paragraph B (and C)

3b B (A doesn't fit grammatically, C doesn't fit with the meaning in the text)

4   2 inhabitants 3 objects 4 rise 5 disappearance

5   2 survival 3 evidence 4 production 5 differences

6   2 B 3 A 4 A 5 B

Global gardening (pages 30–31)

1a/b Students' own answers

2 2 verb **3** noun **4** adverb

3 1 B/D **2** C/G **3** E/H **4** A/F

4 2 C **3** H **4** F

5 2 B **3** D **4** F

6 B 4 **C** 2 **E** 1

7b **a)** a period of time when there is no rain
   b) grow well
   c) an animal / bird / insect which destroys crops or garden plants
   d) at risk

The *Rongorongo* script (pages 32–33)

1a 2 A **3** B **4** C

2 2 B **3** B **4** A **5** A

3a **Suggested answers: b)** A, C, I, L **c)** D, F, J **d)** 4 D, K
   e) B, E (in the sense of 'small forest'), G

4 2 C **3** F **4** K **5** G

5 **a)** gap 3 **b)** gap 4 **c)** gaps 1 and 2

6 1 E **2** H **3** J **4** G

7 **b)** abstract **c)** literacy **d)** widespread
   e) captured **f)** factor

Material origins (pages 34–35)

1a natural: cotton, silk, wool
   man-made: nylon, polyester, acrylic

1b 1 wool **2** cotton **3** silk **4** nylon

2 2 D **3** A **4** E **5** B

3 Students' own answers.

4 1 adjective. This is because the gap is immediately before a noun and the text will make sense if there is nothing in the gap.
   2 plural noun. This is because there is the word many and a plural verb (*many of whom* **were**) before the gap.
   3 singular noun. This is because there is the word *a* before the gap.
   4 plural noun. This is because there is the plural verb *were* after the gap.
   5 uncountable noun / *-ing* form. This is because there is no article (*a* or *the*) before the gap but the verb is still singular (*was*).

5 2 weavers **3** mill **4** techniques **5** spying

6 1 waterwheels **2** heating system **3** poison **4** museum

7 **b)** set up **c)** acquire **d)** build up **e)** play

Letting off steam (pages 36–37)

1

	feature	location
Grand Canyon	valley	USA
Angel Falls	waterfall	Venezuela
Mount Everest	mountain	Nepal
Mount Vesuvius	volcano	italy
Quelccaya Ice Cap	glacier	Peru
Old Faithful	geyser	USA

3 1 conduit **2** throat **3** lava **4** parasitic

4a/b Words that appear in the text are: water, geothermal, tourists, steam

5 1 magma **2** superheated **3** hot spring **4** vent **5** silica

6 2 D **3** C **4** E **5** A

7a **b)** irregular **c)** unpredictable **d)** unreliable **e)** inactive
   f) abnormal

Designed for disaster (pages 38–39)

1 Students' own answers.

2 Possible answers
   Section A: a severe earthquake, young designers
   Section B: how earthquakes happen, how earthquakes affect buildings
   Section C: building materials
   Section D: building design, researching & testing
   Section E: a design competition

3 2 E **3** A **4** D **5** B

4b **a** incorrect – more than two words, **b** correct,
   c incorrect – not words from the text

4c 2 seismic waves **3** to side **4** much faster **5** strain

5a (quake-proof) building materials; section C

5b 1 expensive **2** unreinforced **3** low **4** bamboo **5** affordable

Animal intelligence (pages 40–41)

1a/b Students' own answers

2 **Suggested answers**
   a) **A** anatomy **B** anatomy **C** intelligence and anatomy **D** intelligence and behaviour **E** intelligence, behaviour and anatomy **F** intelligence, behaviour and anatomy **G** intelligence
   b) The main focus is on intelligence
   c) All except whether they can recognise their own reflection in a mirror

3a 2 B 3 C 4 C 5 E

3b Students' own answers

3c 2 B 3 A 4 D 5 C

4b 1 D 2 F 3 A 4 B 5 C

Dealing with failure (pages 42–43)

1a/b Students' own answers

2a b) failure c) fails d) succeed e) successful

2b Students' own answers

3a **Suggested answers**
   A It is hard to achieve success without experiencing failure.
   B Sometimes companies do not want to know why something failed.
   C Managers should encourage workers to talk about their failures openly.
   D Staff need to learn to discuss failures but still follow company rules.
   E Failures are an essential part of business development.
   F Experimentation and creative thinking in business should be encouraged.

3b 1 Evelyn Krens 2 aviation industry 3 Six Sigma, 3M 4 Eli Lilly

4a 2 D 3 E 4 F

4b **Suggested answers**
   2 … they are not punished > … no disciplinary action is taken. = a
   … if their mistakes were accidental. > However, this does not apply to cases where staff have deliberately disobeyed rules. = a, c
   3 After the introduction of the Six Sigma at 3M > this company introduced Six Sigma = b
   scientists tended to experiment less > scientists working there lost their willingness to be creative and test out new possibilities for products = a, d
   4 Technique d

5b 1 B 2 A 3 D 4 G 5 F

Harmful to health (pages 44–45)

1 Students' own answers

2 a) Peru b) A large lead mine c) Health problems; people have to leave their homes

3a 2 C 3 E 4 E 5 F i E ii E iii C iv A v F vi C

3b 2 iii, vi 3 i 4 ii 5 v

4 Students' own answers

5a 2 E 3 H 4 H

5b 1 false (people have been forced from their homes because the mine is expanding)
   2 not given (we can guess that some children may have died, but the text doesn't say this)
   3 true
   4 true

6 2 false (even low levels of lead cause damage)
   3 not given (the text mentions the risk to children from dust, but not from water)
   4 false (the text says the mine is now owned by a Peruvian company)

Print your own (pages 46–47)

1 Students' own answers

2a **Suggested answer**
   A 3D printer prints whole objects using (heated / coloured) plastic.

2b Students' own answers

3a boats (*kayak* in paragraph A)
   food (paragraph B)
   mobile phone cases (paragraph D)
   aeroplanes (paragraph E)
   clothes (*shoes* in paragraph E)
   bottles (paragraph E)
   buildings (paragraph E)
   bones (paragraph F)
   body parts (paragraph F)
   human hands (paragraph F)
   TV remote control (paragraph G)

3b **Suggested answers**
   a) Whole object: boat (kayak)*, food, mobile phone case, bones, human hands
   Parts: aeroplanes, boat*
   * He printed all the parts to make the boat
   b) Finished object: boat, food, mobile phone case, bones, human hands
   Model: building, shoes, bottles, body parts
   c) Possible in the future: complete working devices, e.g. TV remote control

4a **b)** large; expensive **c)** smaller; affordable
d) easy / possible **e)** possible **f)** quickly; inexpensively
g) miniature **h)** complicated

5 **1 a** cheaply; **b** inexpensively – similar
2 a free; **b** affordable – different
3 a currently; **b** actually – different

6b **2** false (they can also use metal, ceramic, glass, wood
and sugar) **3** not given **4** false (they are used to create
finished objects and prototypes) **5** true **6** not given (the
text says scientists believe printing complete devices will
be possible eventually, it doesn't say whether they've
already started developing the technology or not)

Picture this (pages 48–49)

1 Students' own answers

2 **Suggested answers**
Selfie-sticks because they could damage the artworks, they
encourage bad manners, they are distracting, and people
don't really look at the artworks if they're taking them.

3 **Negative opinion:** bad manners, complaining,
distracting, miss out, negative incidents, worry
Positive opinion: agree, free publicity, helps, positive

4 Students' own answers

5 **a)** a substance that is very dark; the blackest black
b) Surrey NanoSystems **c)** Anish Kapoor

6 **2** a **3** b **4** b **5** c **6** c

7 **1** yes **2** yes **3** not given **4** yes **5** not given **6** no

Water worries (pages 50–51)

2 **a)** California, USA **b)** a drought / water shortage
c) not watering lawns; taking shorter showers; flushing
the toilet less often

3a **a** A, B, E, F, G, H **b** C, D, E

3b **Suggested answers**
Student A
1 wheat
2 the wheat died because of the hot weather conditions,
the soil became loose as a result of ploughing and
when it was dry and windy, it created huge dust storms

Student B
1 More than 30 kinds of fruits, vegetables and nuts,
including pistachios, grapes, almonds and walnuts.
2 Not enough rainfall or water available to irrigate crops.
Some farmers have planted fewer crops this year.

3c **Suggested answers**
In the 1930s, farmers relied on one crop (wheat) and
on natural rainfall, so the drought had disastrous
consequences. Now, farmers grow many different crops
and they have found some ways to cope with the drought,
e.g. by planting fewer crops so they use less water.

4 **2** a **3** a **4** c **5** a **6** b

5 **b)** due to **c)** rather than **d)** could cause

6a **1** paragraph A **2** paragraph C **3** paragraph E **4** paragraph G
5 paragraph H

6b **1** C **2** A **3** B **4** B **5** A

Helpful microbes (pages 52–53)

1a **Text A**
a) penicillin **b)** as an antibiotic drug to treat infections
Text B
a) yeast **b)** in baking to make bread

2 **Suggested answers:**
Places where microbes are found: skin, arm, stomach,
lungs, armpits, behind the knees, nostrils, heels, eyelashes,
roof of the mouth, teeth, hands, guts, lower intestine
Benefits: help to digest food, produce vitamin K, help
immune system fight disease

3 bacteria, *E. Coli*, fungi, mite, virus

4 **Suggested answers:**
b) microbes **c)** microbes (the "harmless hitchhikers"
and the ones "important for human health") **d)** 10,000
different microbial species **e)** *E. Coli* (bacteria)
f) microbes **g)** people living in the same house

5a Outnumber means there are more of; there are more
microbes than the body's own cells

5b C is correct ('bacteria, fungi and other microscopic
organisms' means the same as 'these microbes')

6 **1** A **2** C **3** C **4** B

Chocolate catastrophe? (pages 54–55)

1 Students' own answers

2a Suggested answers

Pair A

a) chocolate makers, farmers, the ICCO, Peter Läderach

b) chocolate makers (including Mars Inc. and Barry Callebaut) have a negative view

Some farmers / growers have a negative view (re. diseases), some have a more positive view and are trying to develop new strains of cocoa

The research organisation has a positive view

Läderach doesn't express a clear view, but gives information

The ICCO is concerned (about disease), but overall has a positive view

Pair B

a) hot, dry weather; disease; increased consumption

b) farmers have suffered lost crops (due to drought and disease), so are having to try to grow more; chocolate makers are having to pay more for cocoa; the environment is being damaged as farmers clear forest to plant crops; wildlife is being threatened by lost habitat

c) developing new disease-resistant strains of cacao; growing cocoa in other areas of the world as the climate warms

3a/b Suggested answers

a) chocolate makers and the ICCO disagree – chocolate makers are worried about the future (paragraph 1), but the ICCO say there's no reason to worry (paragraph H)

b) the writer criticises cocoa farmers who are cutting down forest and damaging the environment (paragraph D). Note that Peter Läderach describes the situation, but the following sentences containing criticism are not attributed to him, they are the writer's own views.

c) Chocolate makers predict the cocoa deficit will increase in the future (paragraph A)

Consumption in China and India is predicted to rise – no source (paragraph E)

Läderach predicts that cocoa could be grown in new areas (paragraph G)

The ICCO predicts that there will be enough stocks so that chocolate production won't be affected (paragraph H)

4 **a)** 5 options in exercise 5, 7 options in exercise 6

b) 2 answers in exercise 5, 3 answers in exercise 6

5 **1** B, D **2** B, D

6 **1** B, C, E **2** C, E, G

Test 1 Massive meltdown (pages 56–57)

Questions 1–7 **1** F **2** C **3** D **4** B **5** G **6** A **7** E

Questions 8–10 **8** True **9** Not given **10** False

Questions 11–14 **11** waterfalls **12** shrinking **13** twice **14** rise

Test 2 Is screen time making you sick? (pages 58–59)

Questions 1–4 **1** E **2** B **3** D **4** E

Questions 5–8 **5** B **6** A **7** C **8** B

Questions 9–13 **9** sleepy **10** cancer **11** alert **12** avoid **13** screen

Test 3 Save the bees (pages 60–61)

Questions 1–4 **1** B **2** D **3** A **4** C

Questions 5–9 B, D, E, G, I

Questions 10–13 **10** apples, pears **11** 2.7 million **12** by truck **13** about 1/3 / a third

Questions 14 B

Academic Word List

The Academic Word List (AWL) was developed by Averil Coxhead. The list contains 570 word families which commonly appear in academic texts. The list does not include words that are in the most frequent 2000 words of English. The AWL was made so that it could be used by teachers as part of a programme preparing learners for tertiary level study or used by students working alone to learn the words most needed to study at tertiary institutions. For more information, please visit: http://www.victoria.ac.nz/lals/resources/academicwordlist/

The words below are arranged into Sublists. The words in Sublist 1 occur more frequently in academic texts than the other words in the list. Sublist 2 occurs with the next highest frequency, and so on.

All of the reading texts in this book contain a percentage of the words on this list.

Sublist 1

analysis	constitutional	established	indicate	occur	role
approach	context	estimate	individual	percent	section
area	contract	evidence	interpretation	period	sector
assessment	create	export	involved	policy	significant
assume	data	factors	issues	principle	similar
authority	definition	financial	labour	procedure	source
available	derived	formula	legal	process	specific
benefit	distribution	function	legislation	required	structure
concept	economic	identified	major	research	theory
consistent	environment	income	method	response	variables

Sublist 2

achieve	community	design	institute	potential	restricted
acquisition	complex	distinction	investment	previous	security
administration	computer	elements	items	primary	sought
affect	conclusion	equation	journal	purchase	select
appropriate	conduct	evaluation	maintenance	range	site
aspects	consequences	features	normal	region	strategies
assistance	construction	final	obtained	regulations	survey
categories	consumer	focus	participation	relevant	text
chapter	credit	impact	perceived	resident	traditional
commission	cultural	injury	positive	resources	transfer

Sublist 3

alternative	convention	emphasis	interaction	philosophy	sex
circumstances	coordination	ensure	justification	physical	shift
comments	core	excluded	layer	proportion	specified
compensation	corporate	framework	link	published	sufficient
components	corresponding	funds	location	reaction	task
consent	criteria	illustrated	maximum	registered	technical
considerable	deduction	immigration	minorities	reliance	techniques
constant	demonstrate	implies	negative	removed	technology
constraints	document	initial	outcomes	scheme	validity
contribution	dominant	instance	partnership	sequence	volume

Sublist 4

access	communication	error	internal	parallel	resolution
adequate	concentration	ethnic	investigation	parameters	retained
annual	conference	goals	job	phase	series
apparent	contrast	granted	label	predicted	statistics
approximated	cycle	hence	mechanism	principal	status
attitudes	debate	hypothesis	obvious	prior	stress
attributed	despite	implementation	occupational	professional	subsequent
civil	dimensions	implications	option	project	sum
code	domestic	imposed	output	promote	summary
commitment	emerged	integration	overall	regime	undertaken

Sublist 5

academic	consultation	evolution	licence	orientation	styles
adjustment	contact	expansion	logic	perspective	substitution
alter	decline	exposure	marginal	precise	sustainable
amendment	discretion	external	medical	prime	symbolic
aware	draft	facilitate	mental	psychology	target
capacity	enable	fundamental	modified	pursue	transition
challenge	energy	generated	monitoring	ratio	trend
clause	enforcement	generation	network	rejected	version
compounds	entities	image	notion	revenue	welfare
conflict	equivalent	liberal	objective	stability	whereas

Sublist 6

abstract	cited	explicit	inhibition	neutral	trace
accurate	cooperative	federal	initiatives	nevertheless	transformation
acknowledged	discrimination	fees	input	overseas	transport
aggregate	display	flexibility	instructions	preceding	underlying
allocation	diversity	furthermore	intelligence	presumption	utility
assigned	domain	gender	interval	rational	
attached	edition	ignored	lecture	recovery	
author	enhanced	incentive	migration	revealed	
bond	estate	incidence	minimum	scope	
brief	exceed	incorporated	ministry	subsidiary	
capable	expert	index	motivation	tapes	

Sublist 7

adaptation	converted	extract	innovation	quotation	transmission
adults	couple	file	insert	release	ultimately
advocate	decades	finite	intervention	reverse	unique
aid	definite	foundation	isolated	simulation	visible
channel	deny	global	media	solely	voluntary
chemical	differentiation	grade	mode	somewhat	
classical	disposal	guarantee	paradigm	submitted	
comprehensive	dynamic	hierarchical	phenomenon	successive	
comprise	eliminate	identical	priority	survive	
confirmed	empirical	ideology	prohibited	thesis	
contrary	equipment	inferred	publication	topic	

Sublist 8

abandon	clarity	deviation	induced	plus	tension
accompanied	conformity	displacement	inevitably	practitioners	termination
accumulation	commodity	dramatic	infrastructure	predominantly	theme
ambiguous	complement	eventually	inspection	prospect	thereby
appendix	contemporary	exhibit	intensity	radical	uniform
appreciation	contradiction	exploitation	manipulation	random	vehicle
arbitrary	crucial	fluctuations	minimised	reinforced	via
automatically	currency	guidelines	nuclear	restore	virtually
bias	denote	highlighted	offset	revision	widespread
chart	detected	implicit	paragraph	schedule	visual

Sublist 9

accommodation	concurrent	founded	norms	route
analogous	confined	inherent	overlap	scenario
anticipated	controversy	insights	passive	sphere
assurance	conversely	integral	portion	subordinate
attained	device	intermediate	preliminary	supplementary
behalf	devoted	manual	protocol	suspended
bulk	diminished	mature	qualitative	team
ceases	distorted/distortion - equal figures	mediation	refine	temporary
coherence	duration	medium	relaxed	trigger
coincide	erosion	military	restraints	unified
commenced	ethical	minimal	revolution	violation
incompatible	format	mutual	rigid	vision

Sublist 10

adjacent	convinced	intrinsic	ongoing	undergo
albeit	depression	invoked	panel	whereby
assembly	encountered	levy	persistent	
collapse	enormous	likewise	posed	
colleagues	forthcoming	nonetheless	reluctant	
compiled	inclination	notwithstanding	socalled	
conceived	integrity	odd	straightforward	

Authors: Julie Moore and Norman Whitby

Publisher: Jacquie Bloese

Packager: CreatEd and associated editors

Project manager: Verity Cole at CreatEd

Designer: ROARR design

Cover design: Nicolle Thomas

Picture research: Amparo Escobedo

Illustrators: Pages 21, 36 & 57 ROARR design

The publishers are grateful for permission to reproduce and adapt the following copyright material:
'Internet undersea', Scholastic Math, 16 Jan 2016, © Scholastic Inc.
Academic Word List, © Averil Coxhead

MIX
Paper from responsible sources
FSC® C007785